MURPHY MAKES ART
Basic Principles of Creating a Good Picture

By Nadya Geras-Carson
Drawings By Don Carson

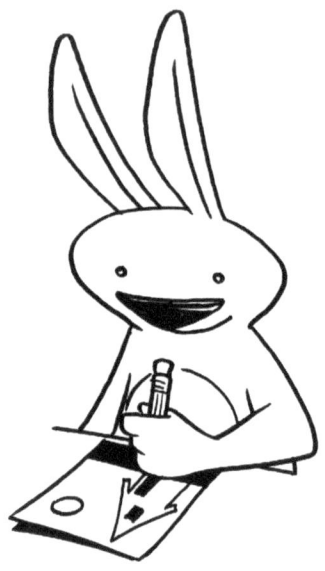

DEDICATION

I would like to dedicate this book to all the teachers that were patient with me, but pushed me to be better than I thought I could be. I would especially like to thank Jon Morgan, Bill Sanchez and Adam Grosowsky, not only for encouragement, but for teaching me all of these basic principles, that are so important. And a special thank you to Adam, for Elephant, Dog, Mouse, and more!

Our thanks and gratitude to Louise Du Cray-Medley, our editor. Without her assistance the reader would have to suffer through a million errors.

I would also like to thank Don Carson, without whom this book could not have been done, not just for Murphy and the wonderful illustrations, but for all the support I could ever want.

NADYA GERAS-CARSON

Copyright © 2018 Nadya Geras-Carson

All rights reserved.
ISBN: 1985690446
ISBN-13: 978-1985690448

Forward

When it comes to creative writing, parents and teachers know that teaching students how to edit and revise written assignments is a necessary skill, but they seldom acknowledge that critiquing, improving, and revising art is just as important. If children don't learn how to critique constructively and how to receive constructive criticism, they will always be oversensitive about their artistic efforts, will never learn how to be positive about others' artistic endeavors, or worse, will be afraid of expressing themselves through any form of art out of fear and feelings of inadequacy regarding their creations.

Don's experience lecturing university students, and Nadya's experience working within college level studios and teaching K-12 art, showed them both that many art students had never been taught basic art principles before being thrown into the deep end of the abstract or expressionist "pool." This left them ill-equipped to handle abstract concepts. University professors often assume their students have had more training in the basics of good design prior to coming to their classes than they frequently have. Simple skills like how to stretch watercolor paper, or how to clean a brush, are often absent from their skill set. It isn't the students' fault. Traditional public schools (as a rule) teach few, if any, basic art skills!

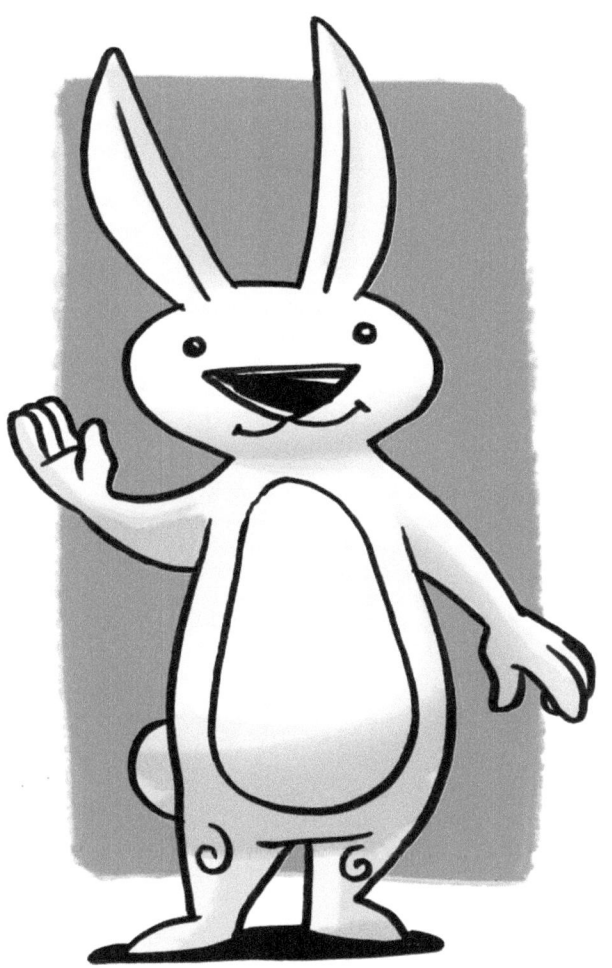

Murphy the Rabbit has always wanted to be a great artist. This book is dedicated to that spirit.

In this book, we will present fundamental skills, which are the basic foundation an artist must have before going on to develop a body of work; like learning scales, intervals, and theory, for musicians, or mastering the alphabet before handling words, sentences, paragraphs, and stories, which are the writer's tools.

The concepts in this book may seem college level, but many elementary students appear to easily comprehend these concepts and vocabulary. We use Murphy the Rabbit as our ambassador to illustrate these basic concepts, not as a way to talk down to the students, but to emphasize that the principles for these lessons are basic and universal. A fifth grader who wants to draw a better dragon and a college student studying art must also master these same concepts.

Oh yes, the students using this book, whether elementary or college level, may also be challenged by some of the vocabulary in this book. We may as well build vocabulary while we are building our design skills.

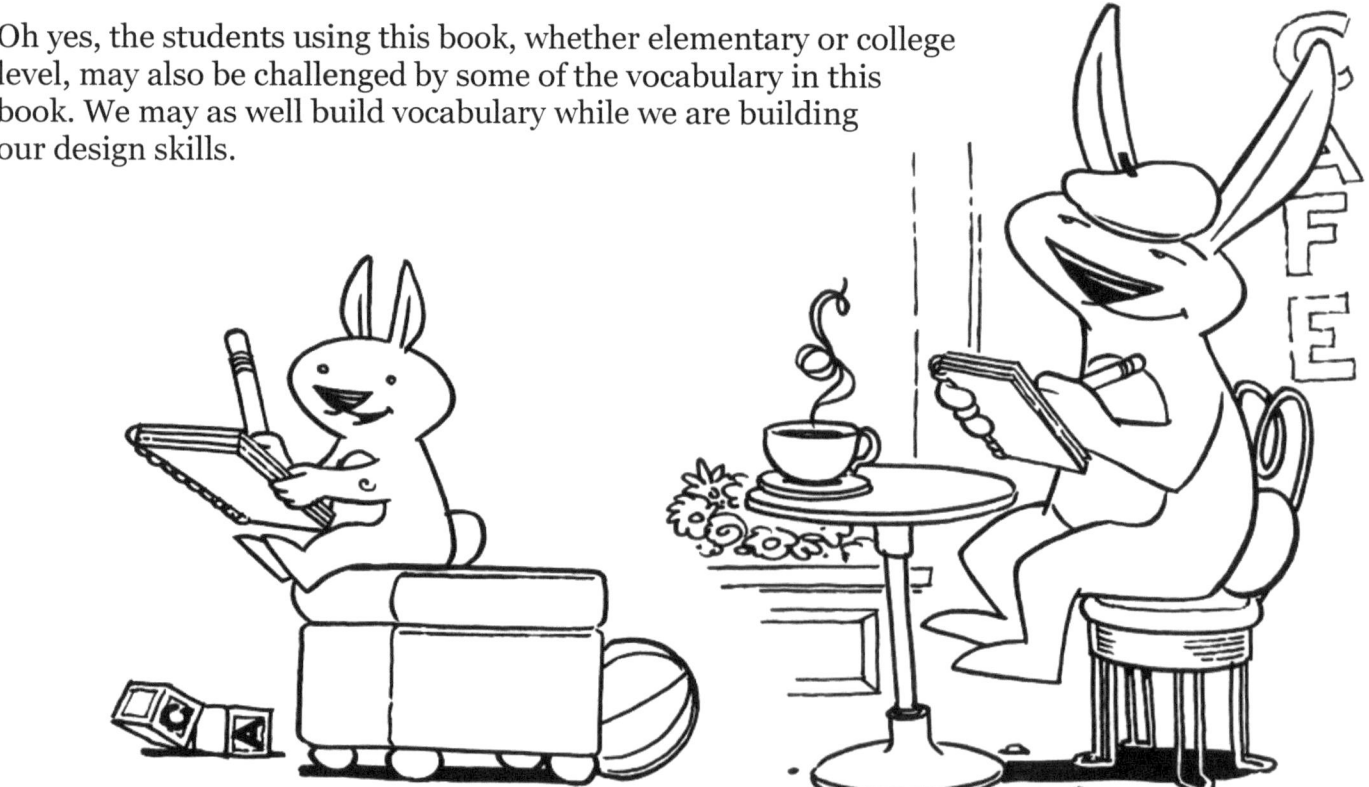

Being an artist is something that can last your whole life long.

Though great artists can, and do, break the rules all the time, they do so with the knowledge of what they are doing, with spectacular results. You must truly know and understand the rules of a concept first before you can break them! These rules will become second nature.

Contained within these pages are many of the beginning tools needed for the ability to design well. It is basically the ten-week class I teach to all ages. We will discuss composition with all its elements, including: value, perspective, placement, pathways, hierarchy of size, and some of those little drawing tricks thrown in too. We will only talk about black and white (with one little exception). Because visual orientation is the goal, we will have many visual examples of each concept. Most of all, this is one subject that most students can absorb with lots of fun thrown in! Mastering drawing, in addition to learning a few tricks, is proportionate to the number of hours an artist puts in drawing. This is true of any life achievement, such as becoming a great cook, or an accomplished musician. Fortunately, if one enjoys making art, these hours add up painlessly.

Some children have drawn since they were old enough to hold a crayon, and spent their free time enjoying putting marks on a paper. Other people come to art later in life, but with the same dedication and energy. They just need to put in those hours too.

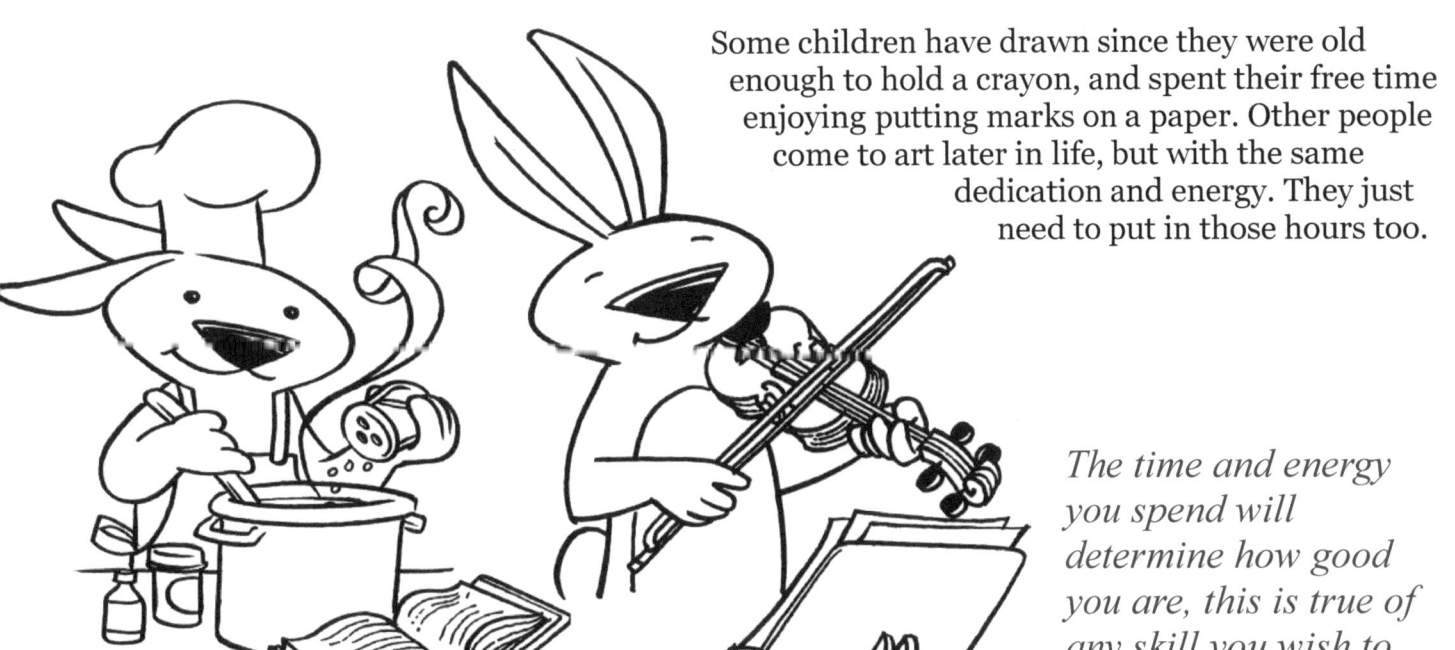

The time and energy you spend will determine how good you are, this is true of any skill you wish to perfect.

If you have never drawn a car or a gorilla before, that object needs to be drawn and completely understood so you can call up that image any time you want. Be good and patient with yourself, and realize time and practice will give you all the tools you need to draw anything you can imagine. Being able to draw well doesn't assure a good finished art piece though. For that you need good design.

It doesn't matter what art supplies you like- the following rules of good design will help you no matter what your style, the medium you use, or your creative field.

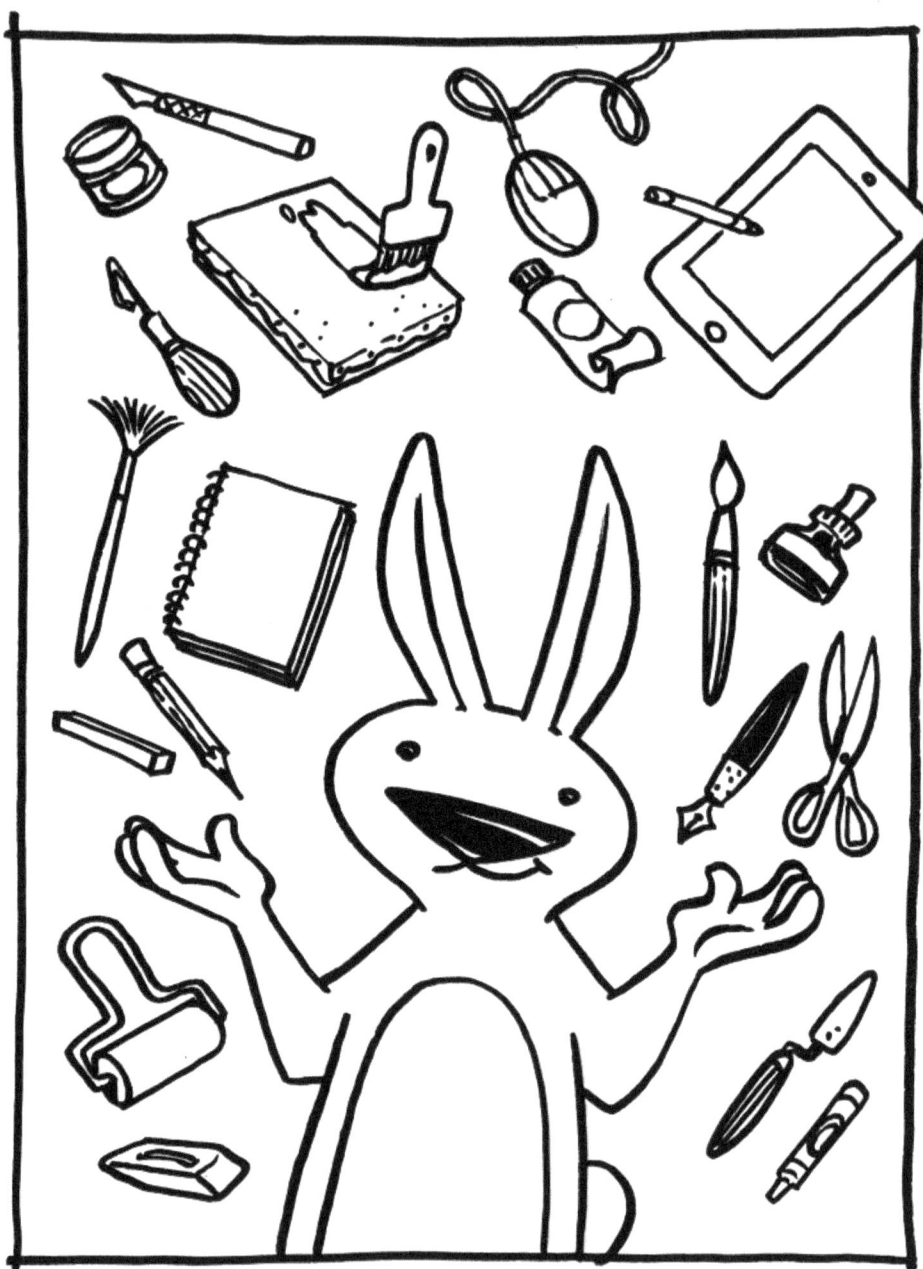

CHAPTER 1
COMPOSITION

One of the biggest components of really great artwork is **Composition**. And yet, this is one element that is frequently lacking in many art pieces, and so diminishes the work.

The dictionary defines composition as:
"The combining of distinct parts or elements to form a whole."

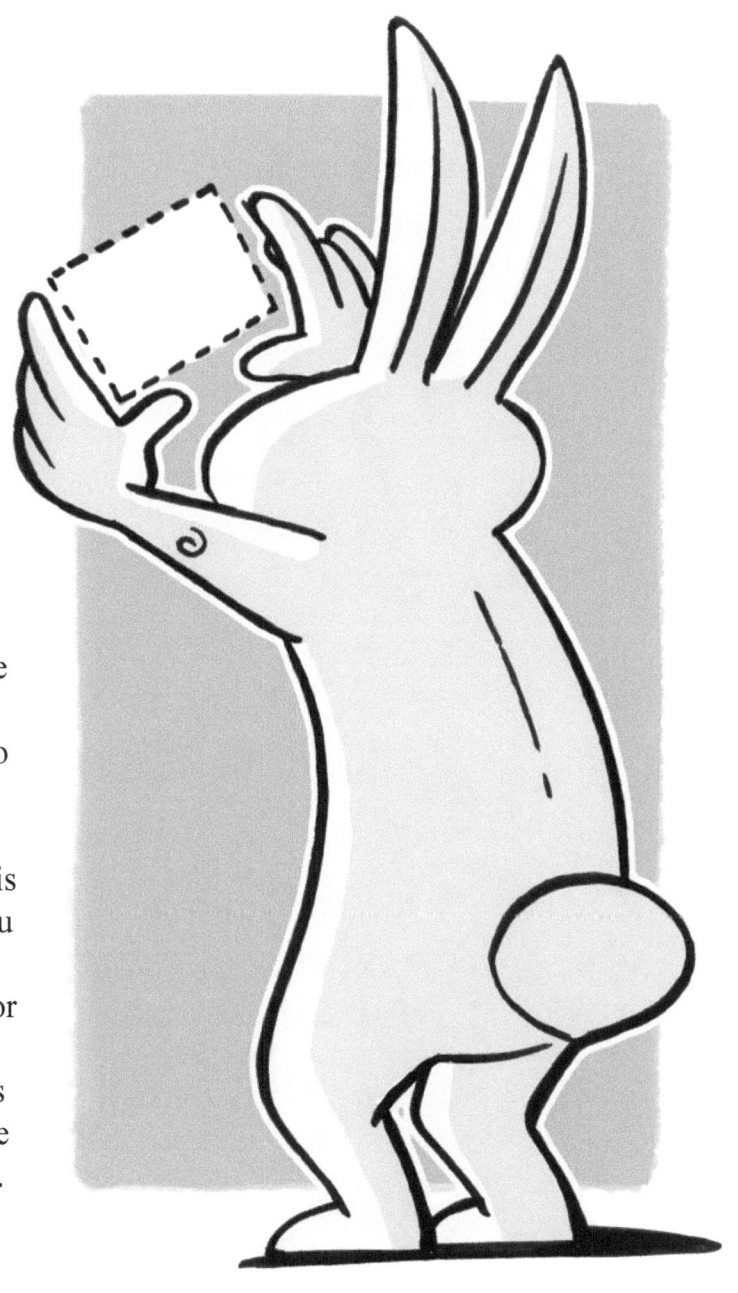

This combination, or "plan" for your piece is the structure, which supports all the drawing, painting, or sculpting in your piece. Your plan to write a compelling story is your outline. In cooking a delicious meal, your plan is your recipe. When you are making music, your plan is the melody or theme that weaves in and out. You can pull many influences into the plan of your creation to give it character-for an artist the color theme in a painting, for a musician the key or tempo of the music, or for a chef the ingredients or temperature in the recipe-but a basic structure on which to build your creation must be chosen. The composition is the arrangement and characteristics of the elements that make the whole.

The composition is the arrangement and characteristics of elements in a **format**.

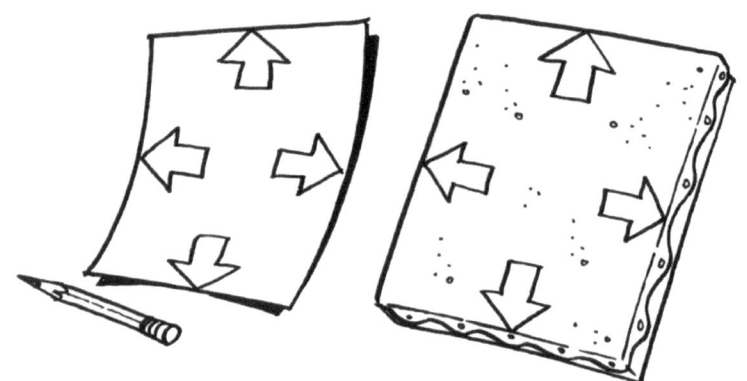

PHYSICAL EDGES of YOUR PICTURE PLANE

A picture plane might be just the natural edges of your piece of paper...

What's a format? A format is the limit or perimeter of your **picture plane**. A **picture plane** is the flat, two-dimensional (height and width) surface on which your art lives. The **format** can be any shape or size, including square, rectangular, round, triangular, narrow, long, short, wide, on a computer screen, on paper, on cloth, on the head of a pin, or on the whole side of a building (which is called a mural). Sculpture also has a picture plane, but it is more complicated, because you have an infinite number of sides and angles one can look at. So we will talk mostly about 2D art right now. Just be aware that composition is as important in sculpture as it is in 2D art- in many ways, even more so.

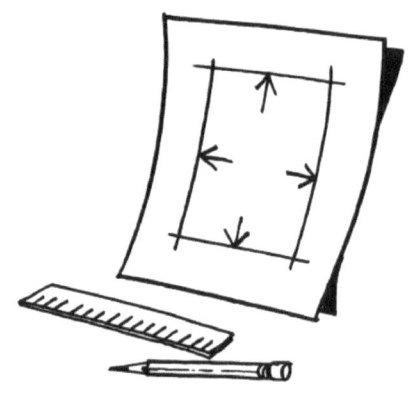

DRAWN BOUNDARIES CREATE A PICTURE PLANE

...or a drawn set of boundaries on any surface.

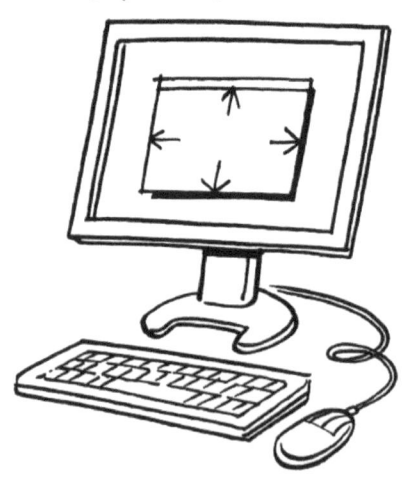

PICTURE PLANE ON A COMPUTER SCREEN

An artist can make any kind of composition, but some compositions can be more interesting than others, especially if you want people to look at your art. A good composition will make viewers look where you want them to, sometimes without the viewer even knowing why.

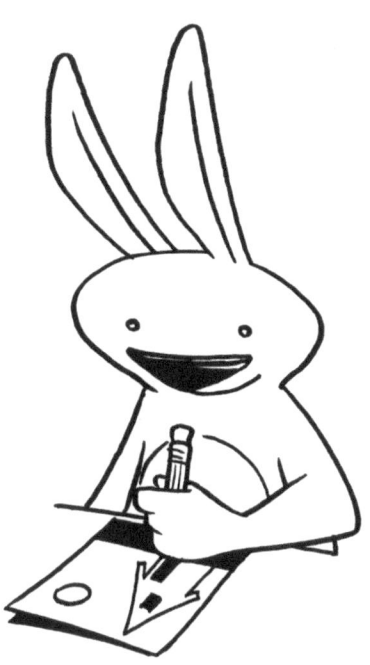

Murphy can draw any picture he likes, but some pictures are more successful then others.

It's like magic! The next time you go to an art show or a museum, look around the room from a distance and pick out the paintings that make you **want** to look at them more closely. These are the pieces that have something exciting going on, and most of that excitement is in the composition.

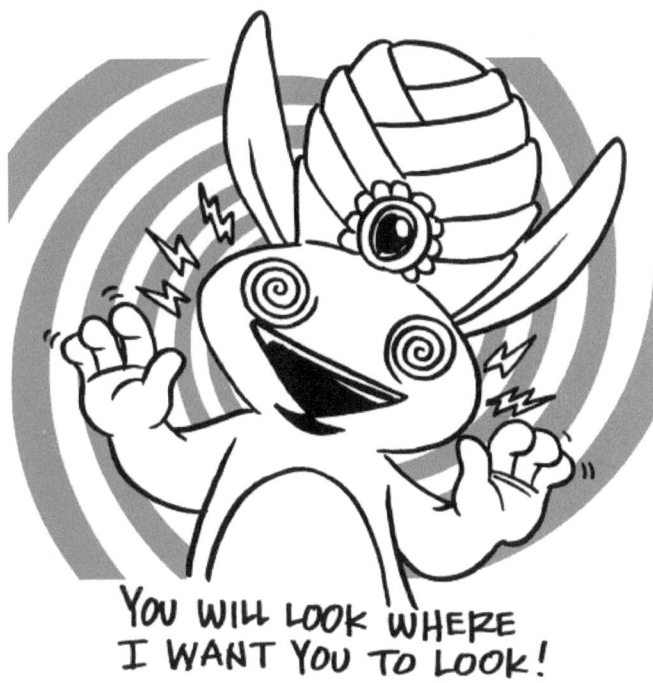

YOU WILL LOOK WHERE I WANT YOU TO LOOK!

Like a magician, the way that you compose your artwork can make your viewer look where you want them to look.

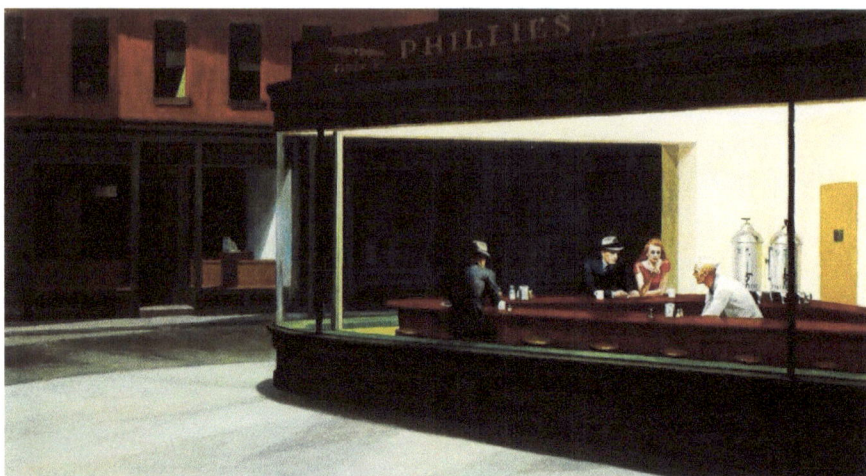

Clockwise: Edward Hopper "Nighthawks" 1942 - The Art Institute of Chicago, USA / **Edouard Manet** "Le Balcon" (The Balcony) 1869 - Musée d'Orsay, Paris, France / **Franz Kline** "Harleman", 1960 - L&M Arts New York

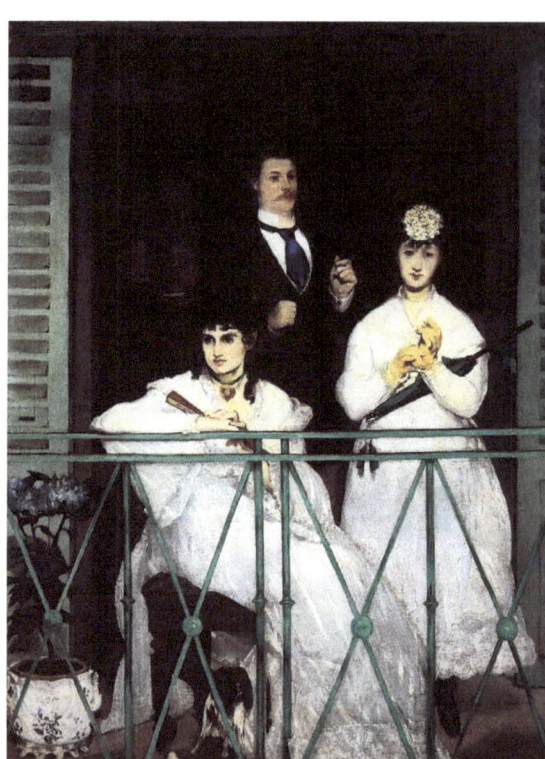

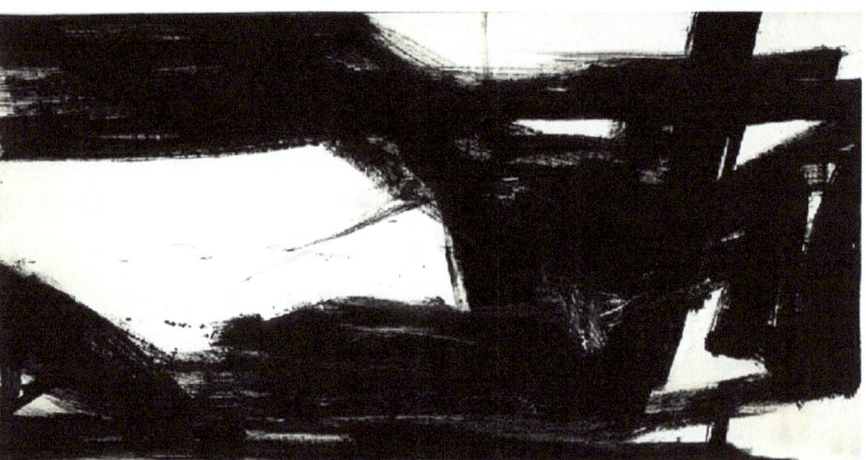

In the next chapter we talk about the individual bones of our structure, composition, and what makes it so exciting.

CHAPTER 2
PLACEMENT

One consideration for your composition is **placement**. Where are you going to put the main elements within your format? We will talk more about placement in chapter 5, **The Rule of Thirds**, but for right now, here are some simple suggestions:

Odd Numbers Are Good
How many objects are in your composition?

One helpful tip: having three objects in your picture plane is not only more interesting than two images, but also any **odd number** of objects is more exciting than an even number. This is another magic trick! This may be why triangles are more compelling, or attention-drawing, than a square. For some reason, peoples' brains respond with curiosity to these odd numbers of elements in a composition.

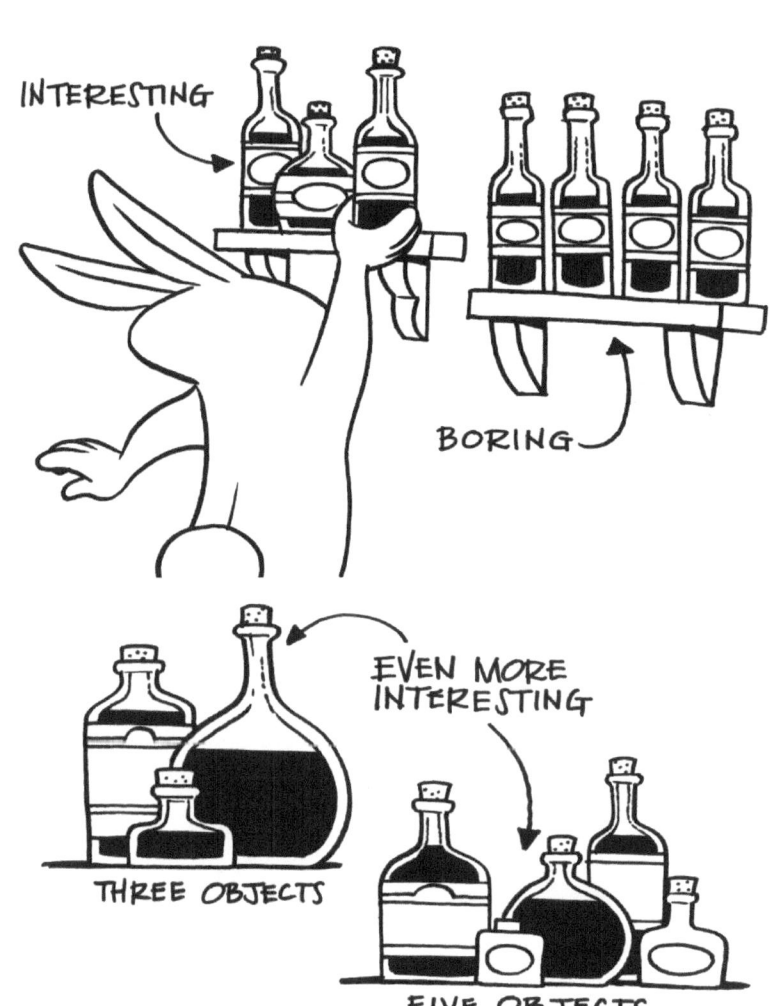

What is the negative space in your composition?

Is the element you are placing a positive space, or a negative space?

Negative space is the element of your picture that contains empty space. Sometimes this can be the most interesting part in your artwork. What is the size of this element? The negative space sometimes may be larger than your positive space

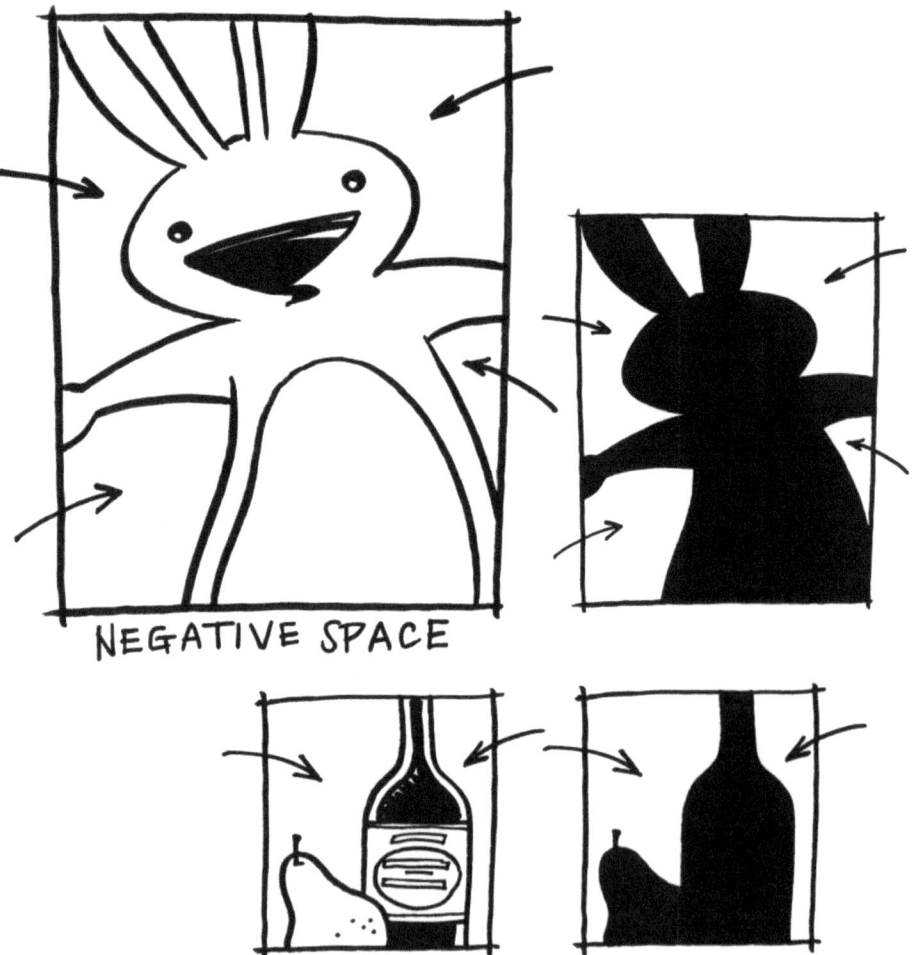

An element can be an object (or positive space), or the space around and in between objects (or negative space).

Bleeding out of the format
Another way to create excitement is to have one or more elements **bleed out of the format**. That means that an element in the image goes beyond the perimeter of the picture plane. For instance, the viewer cannot see one or more elements in its entirety, or an object, or objects extend out of the format. It is peeking out from behind the perimeter of the picture plane. If the artist includes every complete element in the format, there would be no mystery. The viewer's eye is not allowed to complete any of the picture, so the viewer and their imagination becomes bored. Placing one element behind another also creates depth in your format! Look at the difference with Murphy Art:

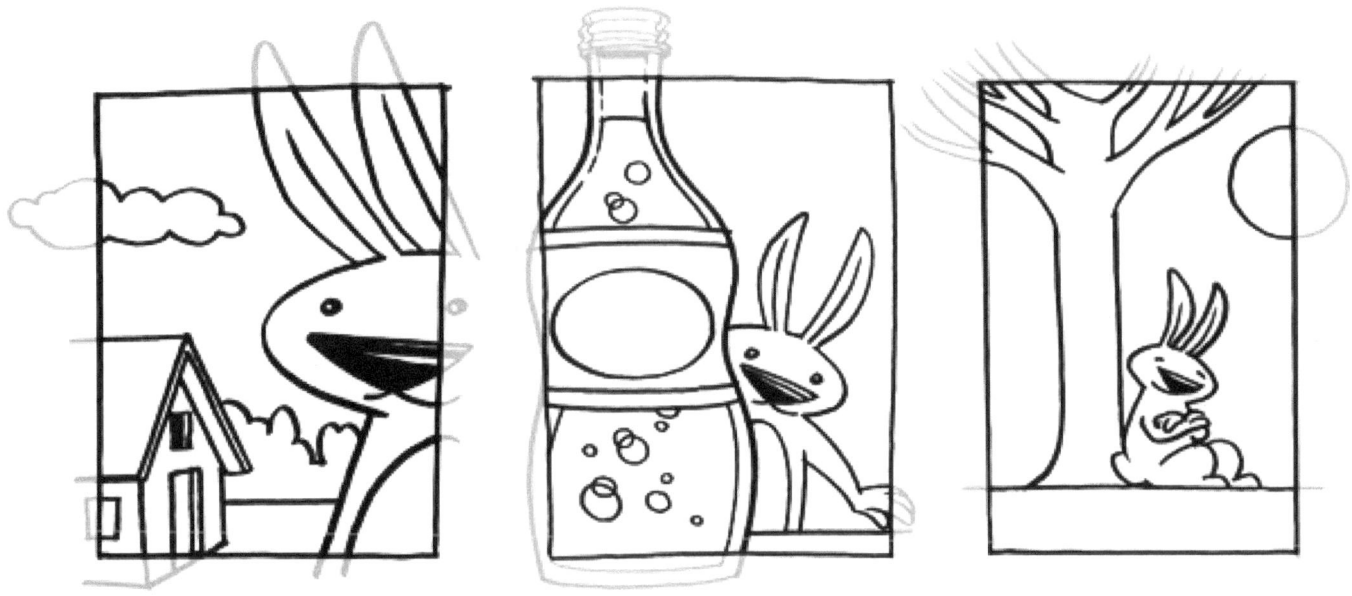

Already we have three design tips in placement! They are: odd numbers of images, negative space, and bleeding out of the format. That's an odd number of secrets, and odd numbers are interesting. This would be a good time to look at some of the art pieces you have been working on to see if these placement tips can be applied to your artwork. You can work right over the top of your piece, making corrections, or use tracing paper to see what a change in composition would do to improve pieces you have done. Most designers use tracing paper (sometimes called flimsy) often, not to copy another artist's drawing or photograph, but to help them explore possibilities in their own compositions. Tracing paper comes in pads, sheets and rolls, so you can use it on just about any size piece.

CHAPTER 3
Hierarchy of Size
or Elephant, Dog & Mouse

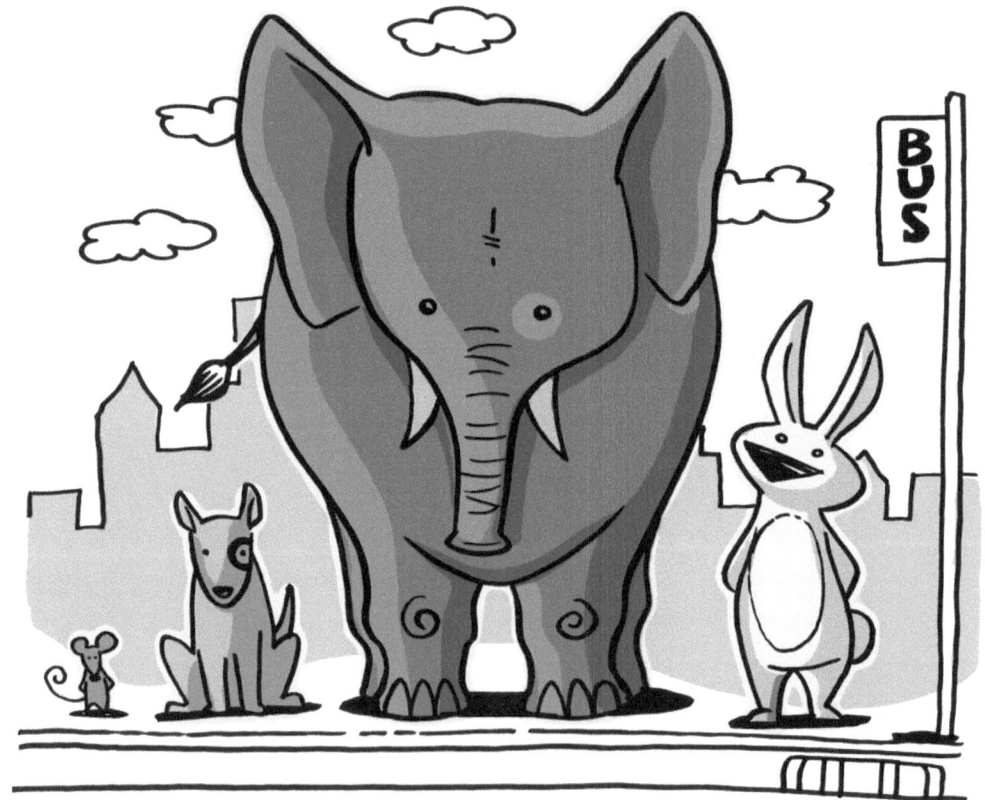

Hierarchy of size is the relative size of an element compared to other elements in your format. There are many possibilities and choices to make whenever you create a work of art. Each decision affects the outcome of the piece, and each aspect is equally important to the finished work. One of your big decisions is regarding the relationship of the elements in your composition, or the design principle which can be called hierarchy of size, but for now, we will sometimes call it **Elephant, Dog & Mouse**.

This is the relationship of the elements that will go into your piece. If the size of all your elements are the same, your art piece will be boring! So you must vary the sizes of each element. One really big element may cover half of your picture plane: a sky, a big close-up of a flowerpot, the bottom of a dancer's shoe, or an elephant! One medium-sized element in your format, about a quarter of your picture plane, may be the size of a dog compared to an elephant. And the third may be the size of a mouse in comparison. This could be a bug on the flower, a bow on the shoe, or a tiny cloud in the large sky. These images can be in the background too, like a mountain, a herd of horses, or a football field. The shape can even be blank negative space. Here is an example: a towering mansion (elephant), with one large window (dog), and a cat on the windowsill (mouse).

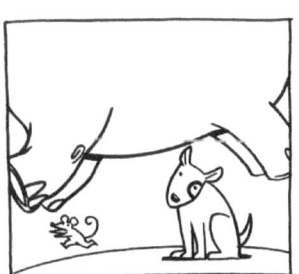 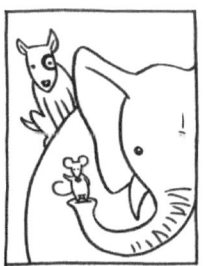 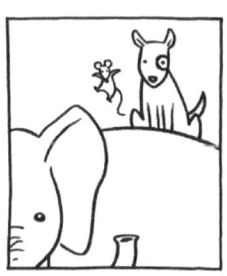

You don't need to include one element of each different size in every art composition. You can make one elephant with many mice like the jewelry on a model for a portrait. The negative space around the model is another element. The mouse can be a point of focus, or many mice can make the composition richer by drawing focus to another point in your piece. You can do the same with all sizes of elements.

Be aware of creating another large shape with your "mice". For example, we have all seen the classic cartoon gag of the swarm of bees becoming an arrow, a huge black cloud, or a tornado. Your group of tiny bees can become an elephant in your hierarchy of size. To use mice in a tiny way, think about small accents, like tiny twinkling stars, leading the viewers eye around a composition, or maybe, bells on a jesters hat that lead to his gleaming eye.

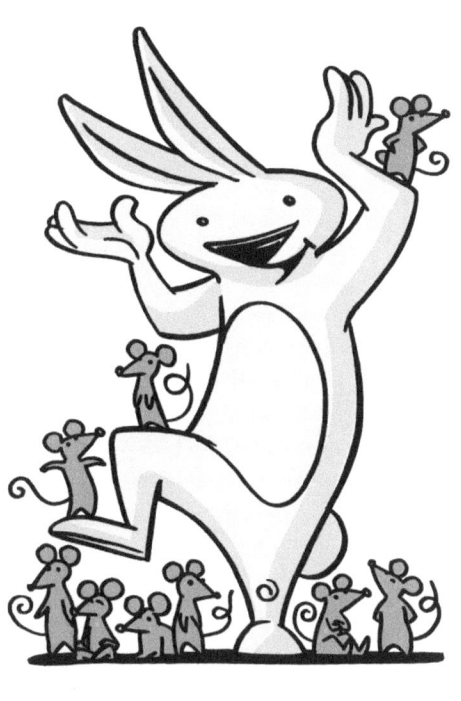

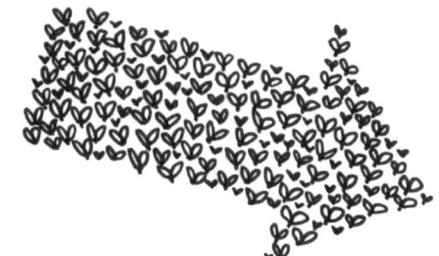

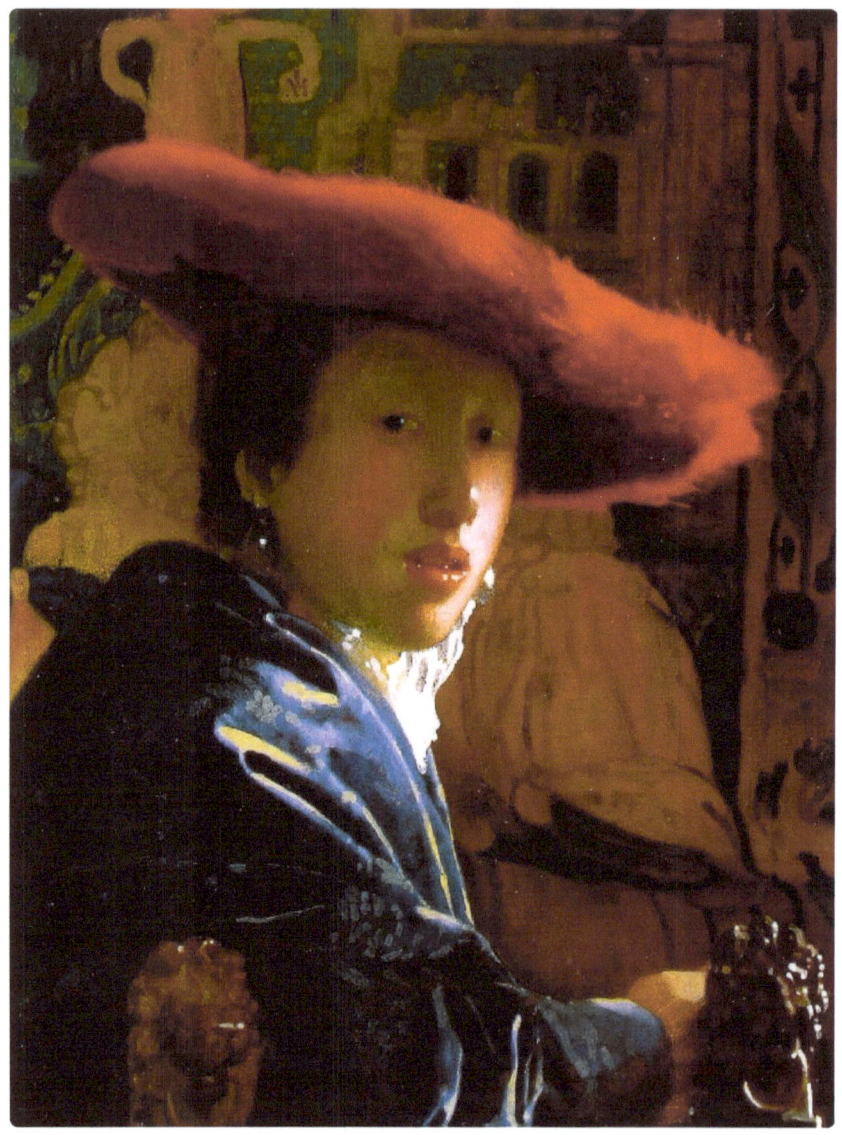

The Girl with The Red Hat, ca. 1665-1666 - National Gallery of Art

In Vermeer's "The Girl with a Red Hat", the highlights lead up her sleeve to the white at her throat, then to the highlights on her earrings and her nose, constantly bringing one's eye back to her face. A good example of Elephant, Dog & Mouse or hierarchy of size.

CHAPTER 4

Pathways & Arrows, Asymmetry & Balance

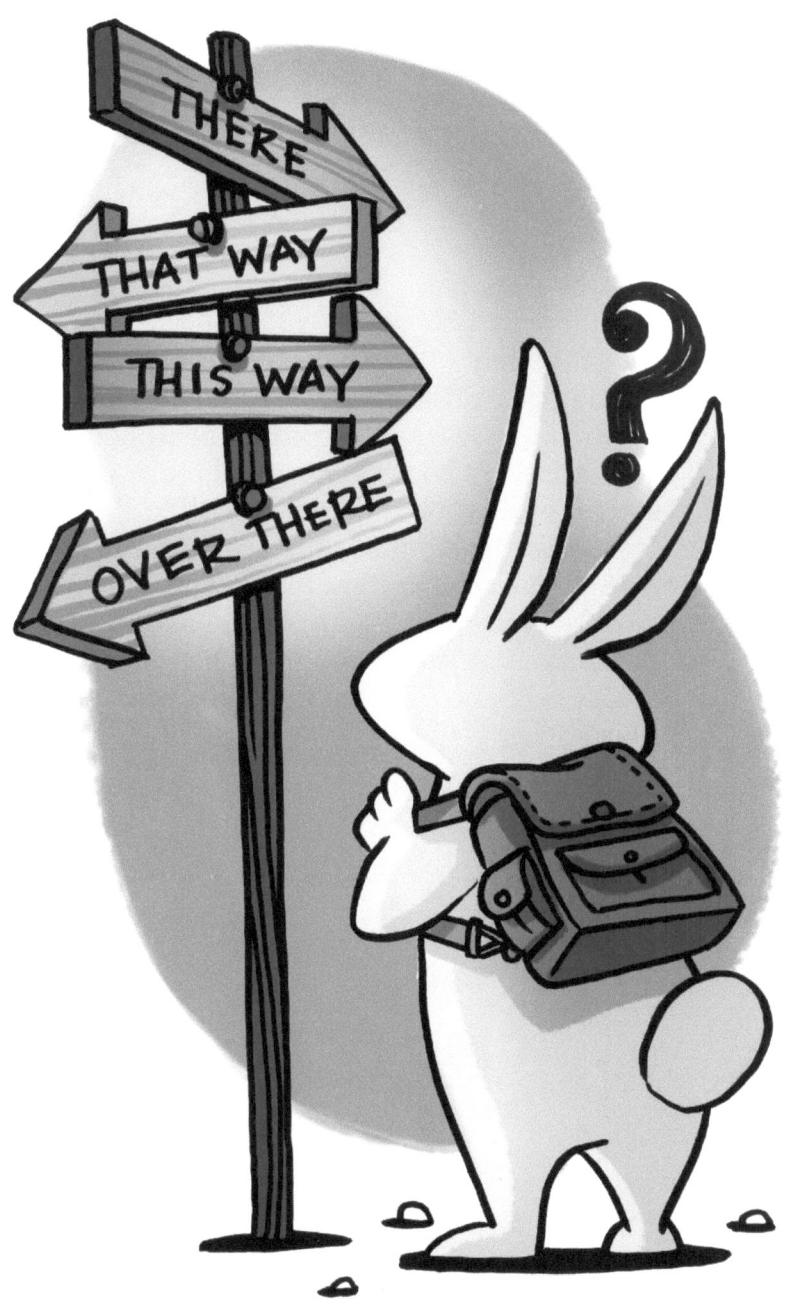

Arrows and pathways are exactly what they sound like- a way to make the viewer of your art look where you want them to look. If you are wandering, lost in a forest, and you see a sign that says This Way Out, or Go This Way For Food, or even I Wouldn't Go This Way If I Were You! (who could resist checking that one out!), the creator of those signs could pretty much lead you in circles- and that is exactly what you, as the artist, may want to do.

The pathways and arrows you set up in your artwork can do the same thing with your viewers. One of the great artists that made use of arrows was N. C. Wyeth. Here is one example of his brilliant orchestration in a painting. It is entitled Blind Pew, and was an illustration for Robert Louis Stevenson's book Treasure Island. Look at all the arrows that point to Blind Pew's face, which Wyeth wanted to be your first focus. The composition makes you continue to come back to it over and over again. Many other compositional rules work here too. See if you can spot them all, and refer back to this after you go through chapter 6, Value.

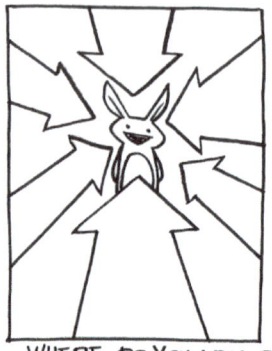

WHERE DO YOU LOOK?

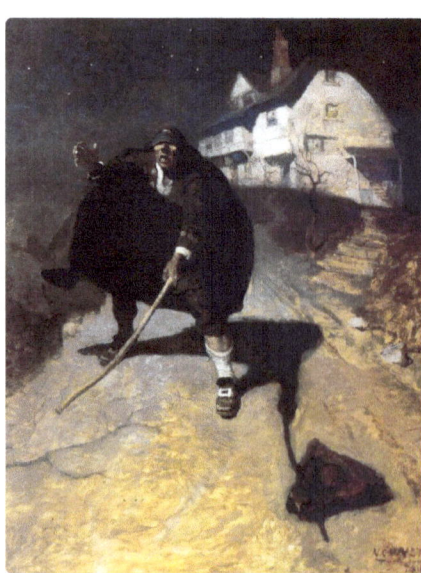

Blind Pew, 1887, by **N. C. Wyeth**

The goal of a good composition is both to capture a viewer's attention, and keep the viewer exploring that work. This is accomplished by moving their gaze around in a continuing pattern within the piece, and always bringing them back to the main focus. A pathway works **exactly** the same as an arrow. The path the viewer's eye takes is swept through the piece, pausing to linger now and then, but always brought to the original main focus. This can be achieved with literal paths.

Here you can see how each line in the composition points to the face of the subject.

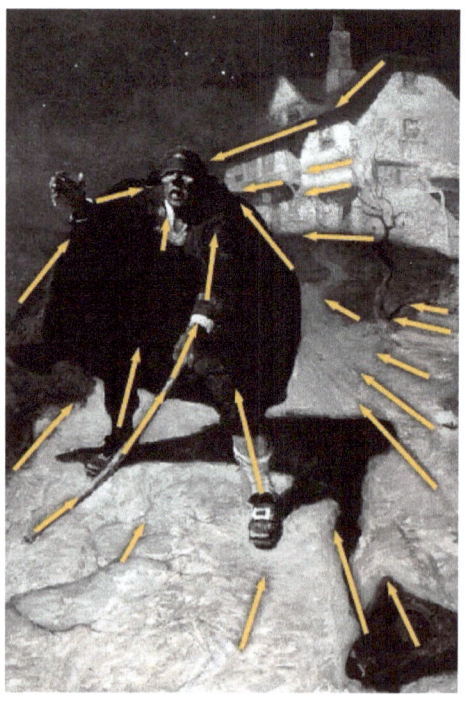

The triangle is used in many classical art pieces to create a balanced composition. You could also use other geometric shapes as a basis for your design.

See if you can find strong shapes in these paintings.

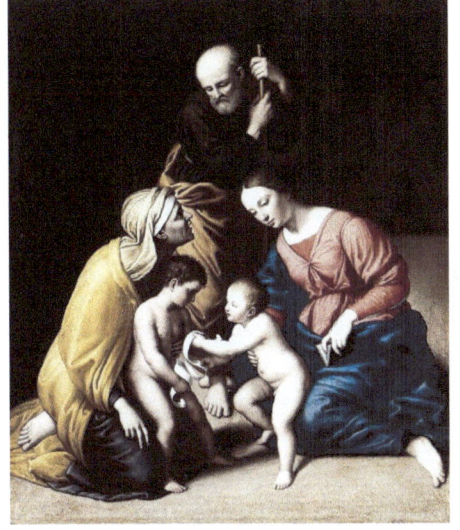
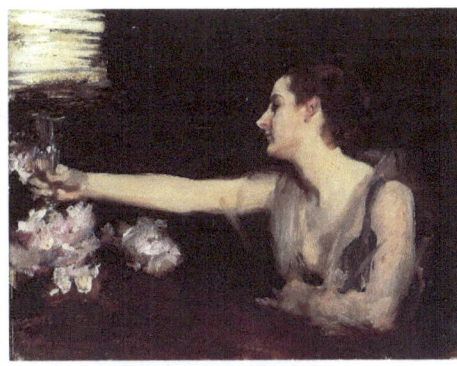
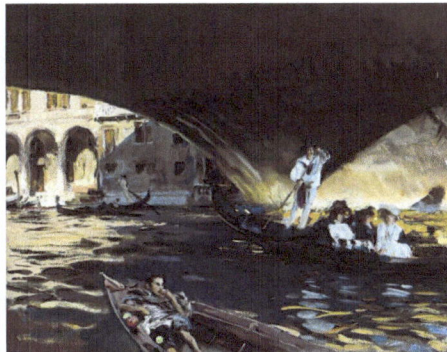
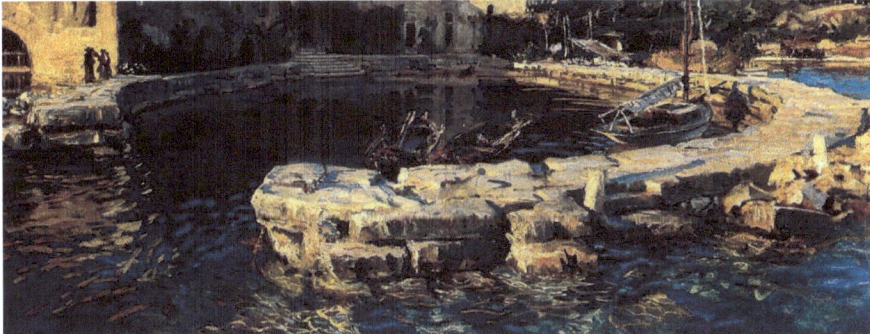
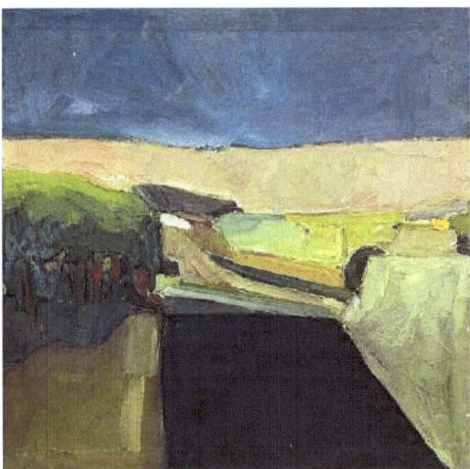

Clockwise: ***Giovanni Battista Salvi da Sassoferrato***, *first half of 17th century, Holy Family with the Infant St John the Baptist and St Elizabeth - Private Collection /* **John Singer Sargent**, *Madame Gautreau Drinking a Toast 1883 - Isabella Stewart Gardner Museum, Boston, MA, USA /* **John Singer Sargent**, *Noho Modern Gallery, The Rialto Venice 1909 - Private Collection /* **Richard Diebenkorn** *(Henry Villierme?), Landscape, 1957 /* **John Singer Sargent**, *San Vigilio, Lake Garda, 1913 - Lord*

Some compositions can be constructed with shapes that the eye naturally follows. The curves of an S, a C, or an X will draw the eye, as will any letters of the alphabet, if they are balanced well. Think about one shape we have talked about before, the stable triangle!

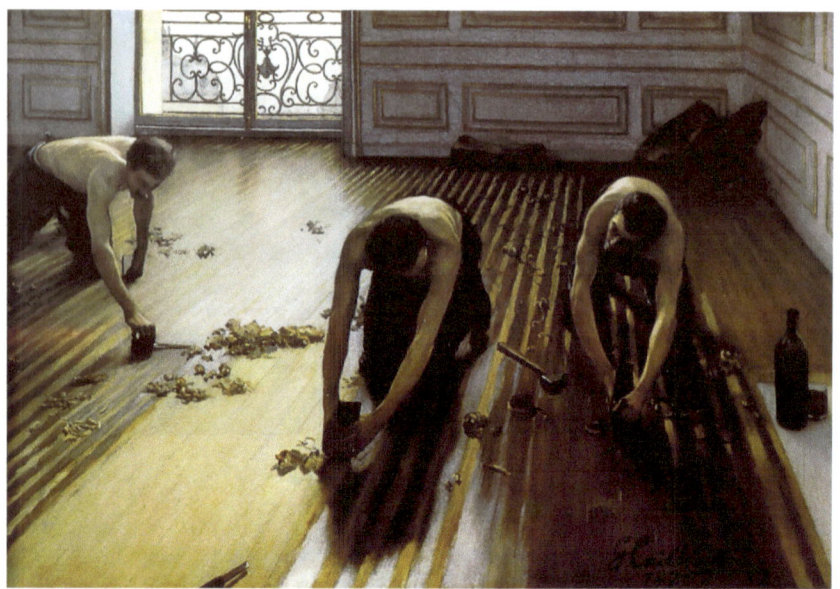

Examples of arrows & pathways in famous paintings.

If you look carefully, you will often find in both beautifully designed art, and in nature, repeating shapes. One example of this is in people's faces. If you see someone with chevron shaped eyebrows, you will notice that their eyes, their mouth, the bottom of their nose, and sometimes even the shape of their hair will also repeat that same chevron shape. Circles, triangles, squares, the letter 'c', or even a peculiar squiggle shape may be present throughout a person, a tree, a sculpture, a building, or anything else you might see. Keep watch for these repeating shapes.

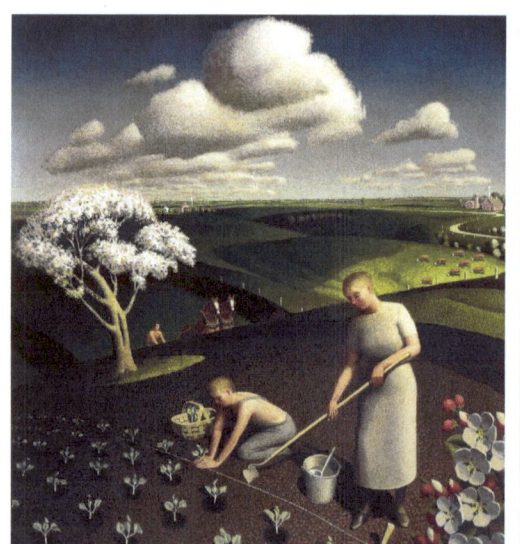
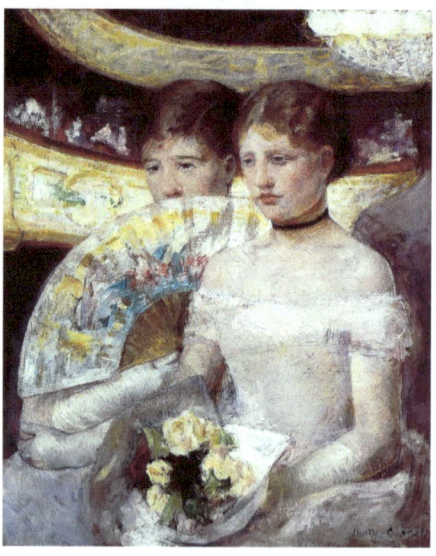

Clockwise: **Gustave Caillebotte**, The Parquet Planers, 1875 - Musée d'Orsay, Paris, France / **Mary Cassatt**, The Loge, 1880 - National Gallery of Art / **Grant Wood**, Spring in the Country, 1941 Cedar Rapids Museum of Art

BALANCE & ASYMMETRY

Now we come to a design possibility that is the choice of two opposites. One possibility is **symmetry**, or balance, and the other is not the other is **asymmetry** - not balanced. Think of your composition as having two dogs, the same size and weight, on either side of a teeter-totter. The teeter-totter is level, and everything is even. This is symmetrical, - it is balanced.

That may be just what you want for a border on a page, or for something else that calls for decoration. Now what happens if an elephant takes the place of the dog on the right? The elephant will go bump on the ground, but the composition is very interesting now! We have an elephant on the ground and a dog in the air, so we have asymmetry, because they are not balanced, and we have objects of at least two different sizes.

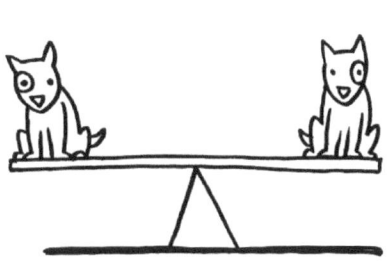

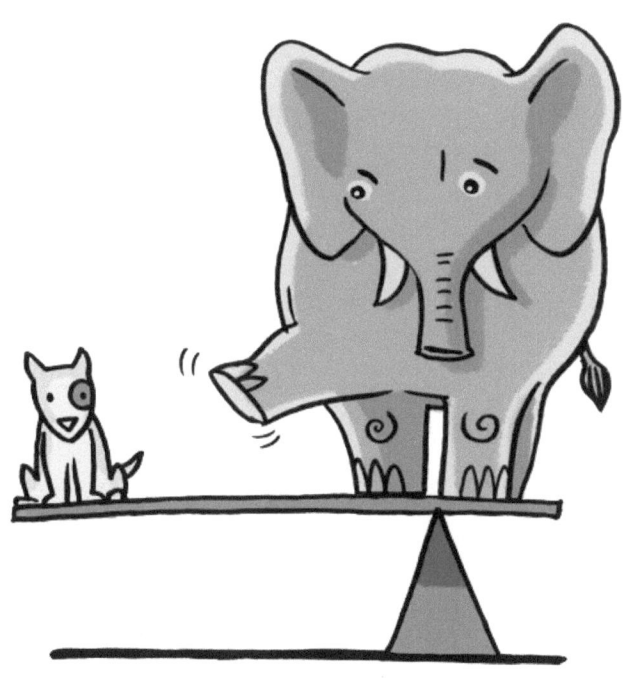

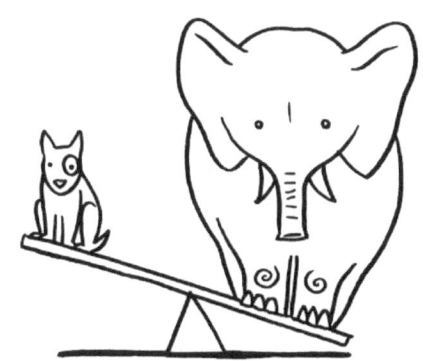

We can fix that unbalanced state by making the board of the teeter-totter move away from the center point, and lengthen the dog's side on the left. The teeter-totter is now balanced, even though it isn't even, which is still more interesting, because it causes tension. What will happen if we move the elephant just a little to the left? Can you try to balance them? What if a mouse takes the elephant's place?

There are many ways to balance a picture. You just need to look at your composition to see if it is interesting. Watch out for anything that repeats itself, like several objects of the same size or the same height in the format, evenly spaced objects, everything horizontal or vertical, everything round, or skinny, or fat, etc. They say variety is the spice of life they say, which is very true in composition, but don't start throwing in as many elements as you can! One designer, Mies Van Der Roh, said "Less is more," meaning keep things simple, clean, and well thought out, not cluttered.

Photographers are some of the best at using these principles, because they have to design within each camera shot. Today, they can change composition digitally in a computer, using programs like Photoshop, but all the design principles we are using still apply.

I had a wonderful teacher who let his class look at 3 or 4 famous paintings each time we met, and we were asked to draw out just the shapes to analyze the Elephant, Dog, and Mouse. Practicing drawing out shapes is one of the best ways to improve your drawing and design ability. Try it with some of your favorite works of art, including sculpture.

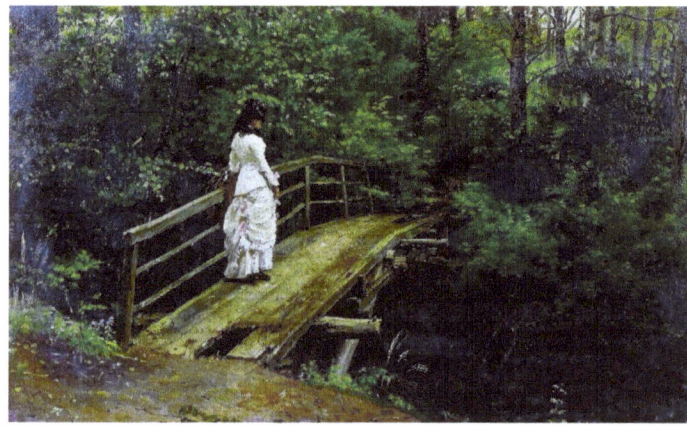

Ilya Repin, On a Bridge in Abramtsevo, 1879, Pushkin Museum of Fine ars, Moscow

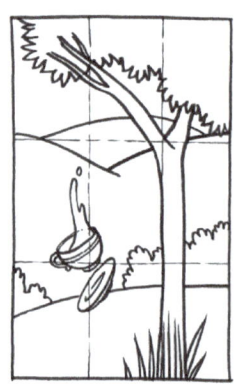 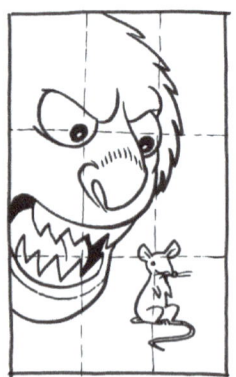

We have been examining what to do with the elements in a composition- but just like a recipe, you need to make decisions about exactly which elements you want to use before you start. If you decide to make a chocolate cake with peanut butter icing, you need to make sure you have all the ingredients, in the right proportions, and mixed with the right companion ingredients. You also need to bake it at the right temperature.

Art rules won't guarantee an art piece will be successful, and going against an art rule doesn't mean a composition will fail, but having guidelines when you are first learning can help a lot. Someday, you will know all these rules without thinking about them. Some rules you might even reject later, but by then you will already have your own aesthetic sense. It has nothing to do with how old you are; it has to do with how long you have studied your field of art.

This would be another great time to stop, take a good look at some of your own pieces of art, and see if you can improve them by applying the last few design principles: Heirarchy of Size, Pathways and Arrows, and Balance and Symmetry/ Asymmetry.

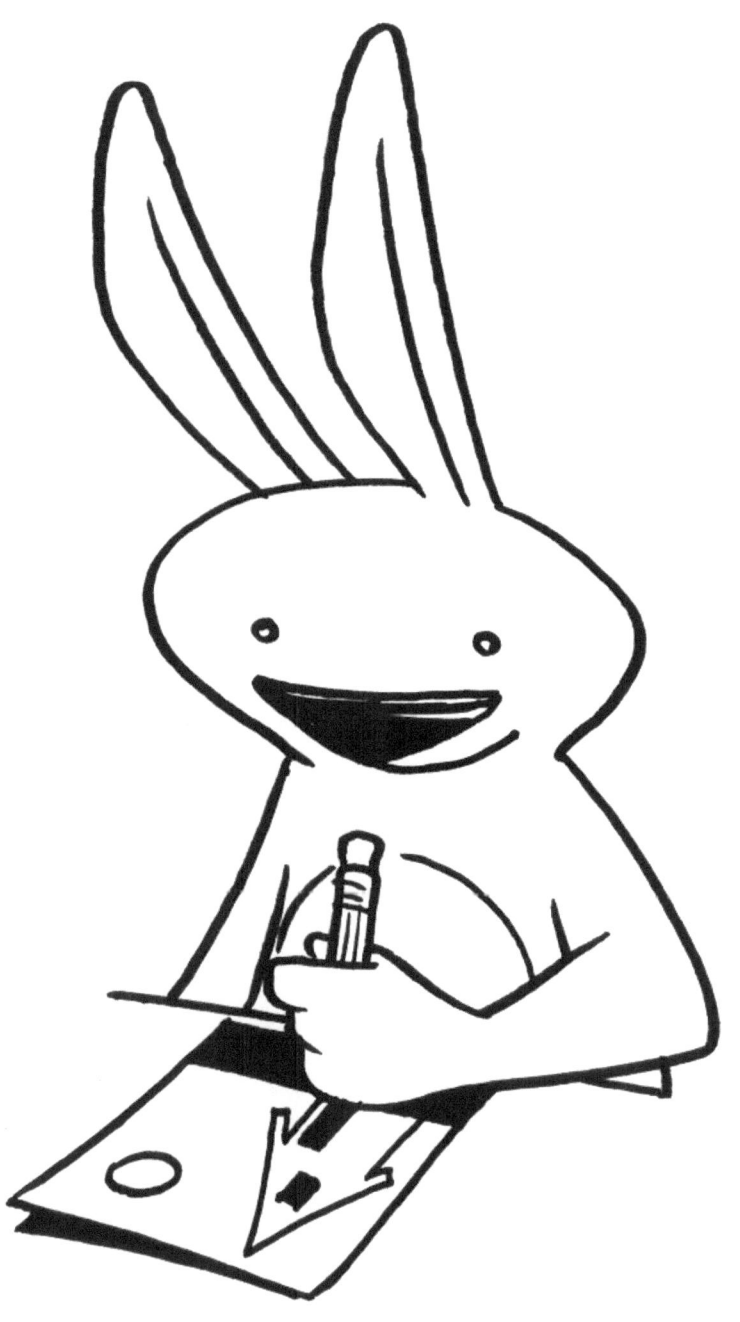

CHAPTER 5
The Rule of Thirds

One valuable composition rule is the **Rule of Thirds**. When an artist uses this rule, it creates four **Sweet Spots**, or points of focus, in every composition. These are places that just make you want to look at that spot. This is a very simple way to place your main focal points, or the object you want people to look at first. These sweet spots can help to lead your viewer into a pathway or story in your picture.

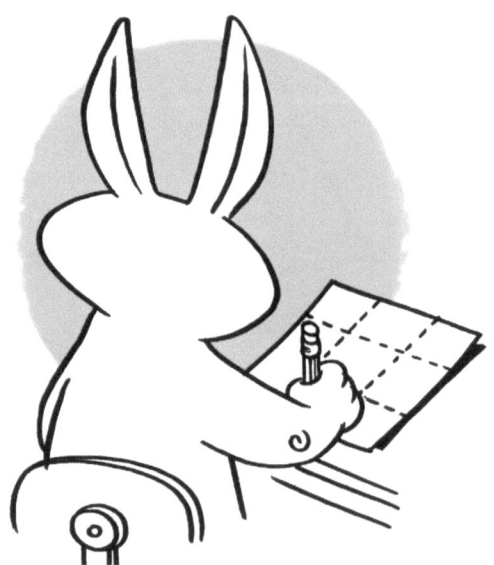
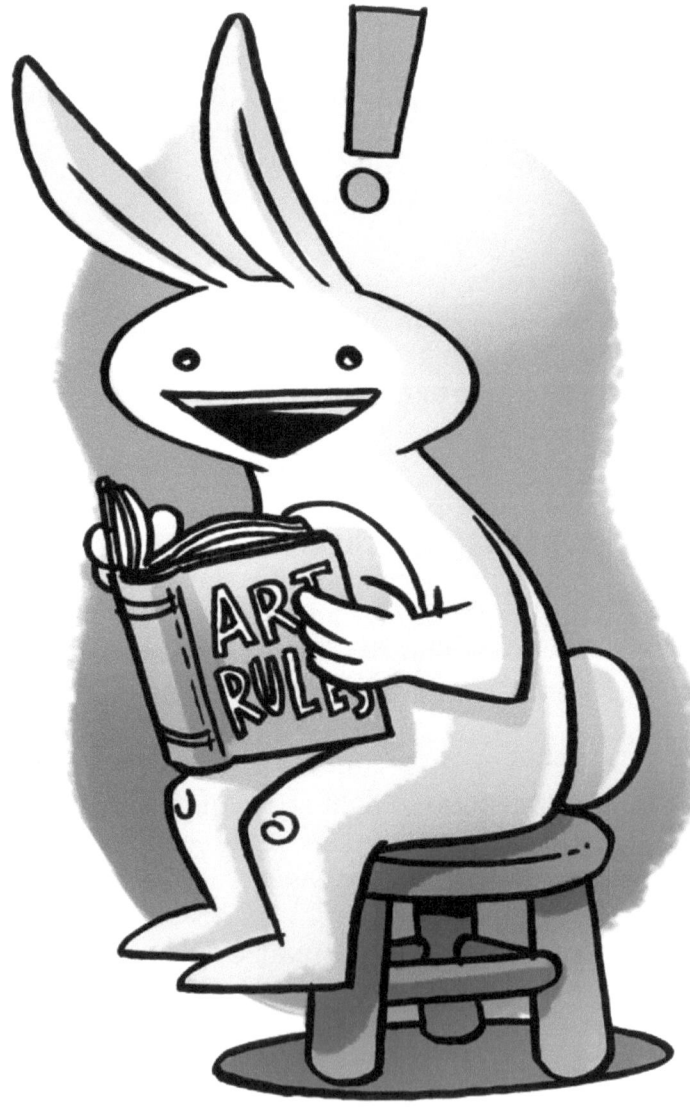

You can find these sweet spots by dividing both sides of your picture plane into three equal parts, and drawing an imaginary line from side to side. Do the same along the top and bottom of your picture plane, and draw a line from top to bottom.

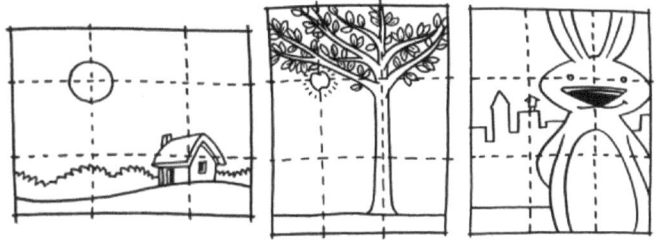

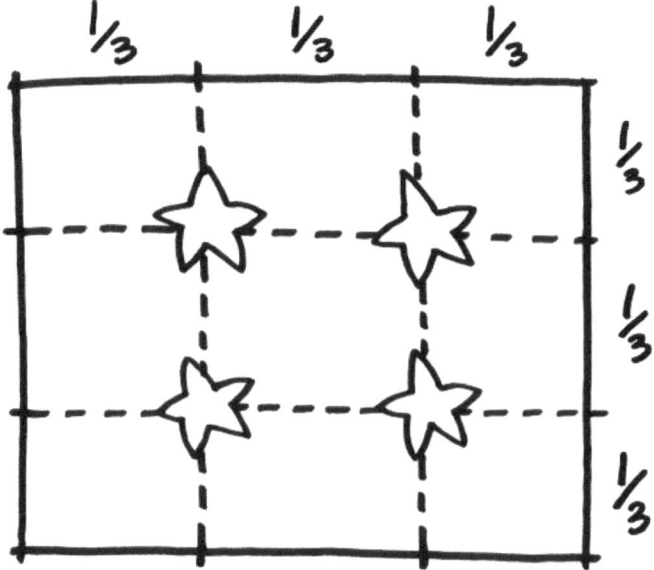

Placing the most important item in your picture on that spot will draw your viewer's eye. Notice that the sweet spot is never in the center of your picture plane.

There is a more precise way to place the focal point, in a perfectly **proportioned** space. Perfectly proportioned means naturally pleasing to the human eye. If the viewer doesn't analyze why it is pleasing, they probably wouldn't be aware of the reason. We find the best examples of this design construction in nature,

Where these lines cross each other, you have the four sweet spots. This is the place in your composition where you might want to place the head of your main subject, the villain sneaking up in the mid-ground, the house in the far background, or the tree that has the golden apple.

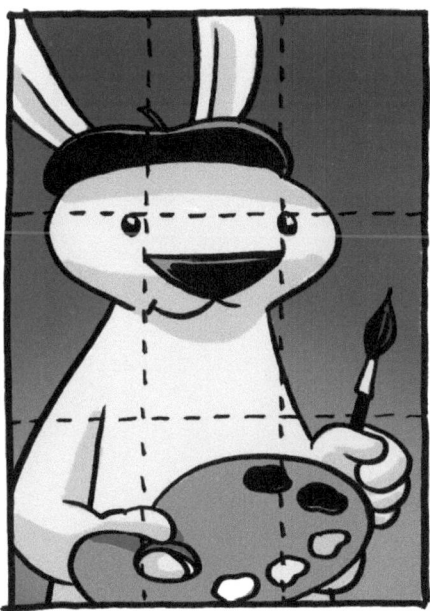

and also in the world of mathematics. In mathematics this is called the golden ratio, and in design we call this measurement the **Golden Section**. I'm sure you have seen it many times in the world around you. It is clearly demonstrated in the chambers of a nautilus shell, the proportion of a fern leaf unfurling, the elliptical orbit of a planet, and even the endless repetition of fractal patterns (Take some time to search information about fractals if you can!).

An easy shortcut, or approximation, to finding the Golden Section is to use a rough estimate of 3/5 to 2/5, or divide a line into five equal parts, with three on one side and two on the other side.

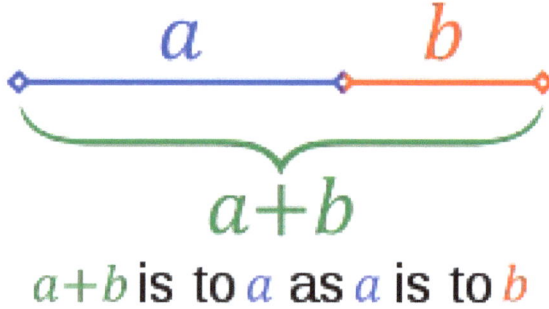

$a+b$ is to a as a is to b

There is a precise way to mathematically find the exact measurement by using the ratio 0.617 to 0.383, or by using geometry (each side divided by 2.62), but for now, it is helpful to just be aware of a perfect proportion when we see it.

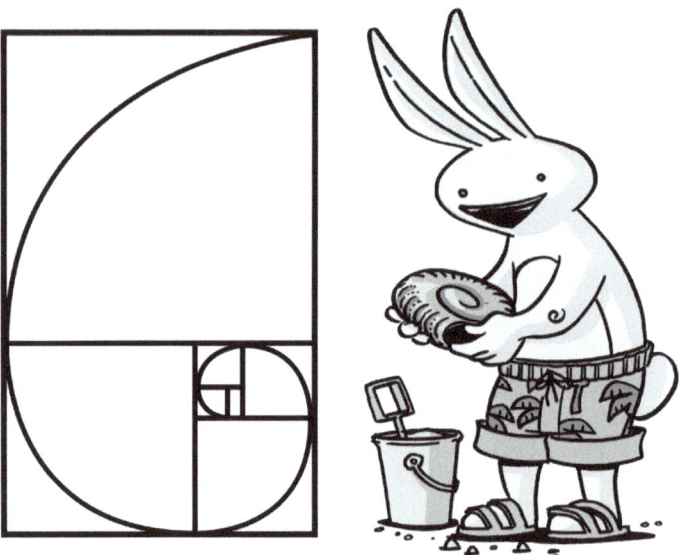

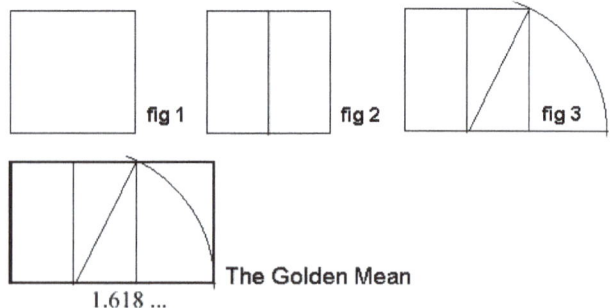

The Golden Mean

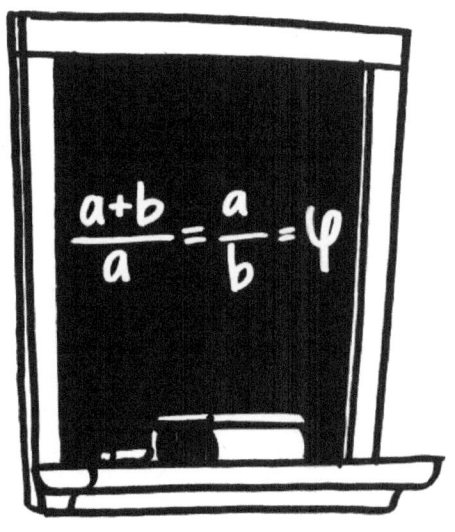

Why are these proportions important? Because the human brain is drawn to them. This shape seems pleasing and right. You can keep dividing your artwork into continuous golden rectangle divisions, and your audience will love the image and not know why! Another piece of magic.

The Golden Rectangle is used in all sorts of good design. Even the architects of the old world understood its importance in their designs.

As you can see, the Golden Section influences more than just works of art. Architecture also uses this rule when designing buildings, such as the Parthenon.

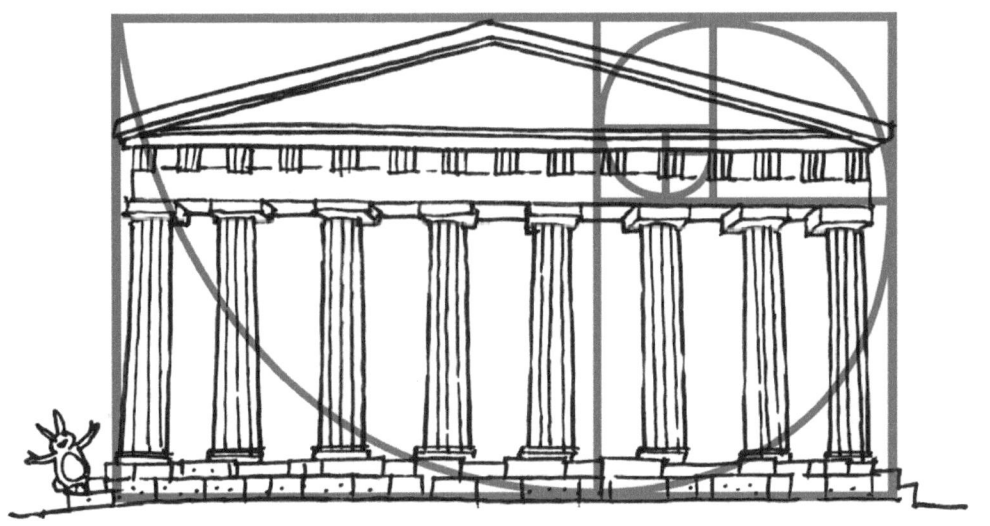

Time to pull out your own compositions to see if you can use the rule of thirds to improve a composition. This might be a good time to try a new composition using all we have discussed so far. We really have used a lot of major principles, so this might be harder than you think.

CHAPTER 6
Value

One of the most important design elements in any art piece is called **Value**. The simplest definition of value in art design is the artist's use of light or dark elements in a piece. Is your elephant gray with a white mouse sitting on his trunk, and a black dog watching? If so, what value is the negative space? Or could a frog be the largest element, with a bright light shining on him, in a dark swamp, with a gray fly on the frog's nose? These are the basic decisions you, as the artist, must make when you are designing.

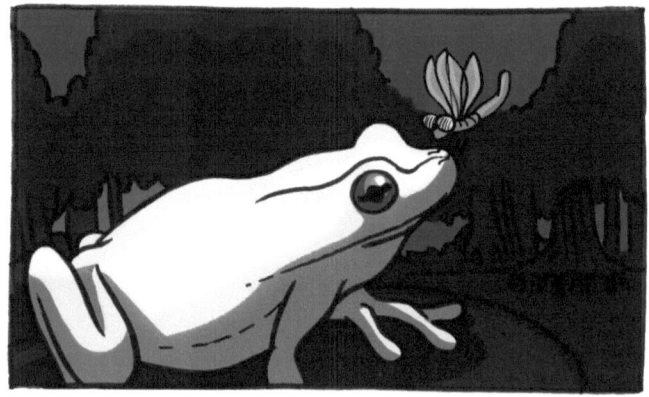

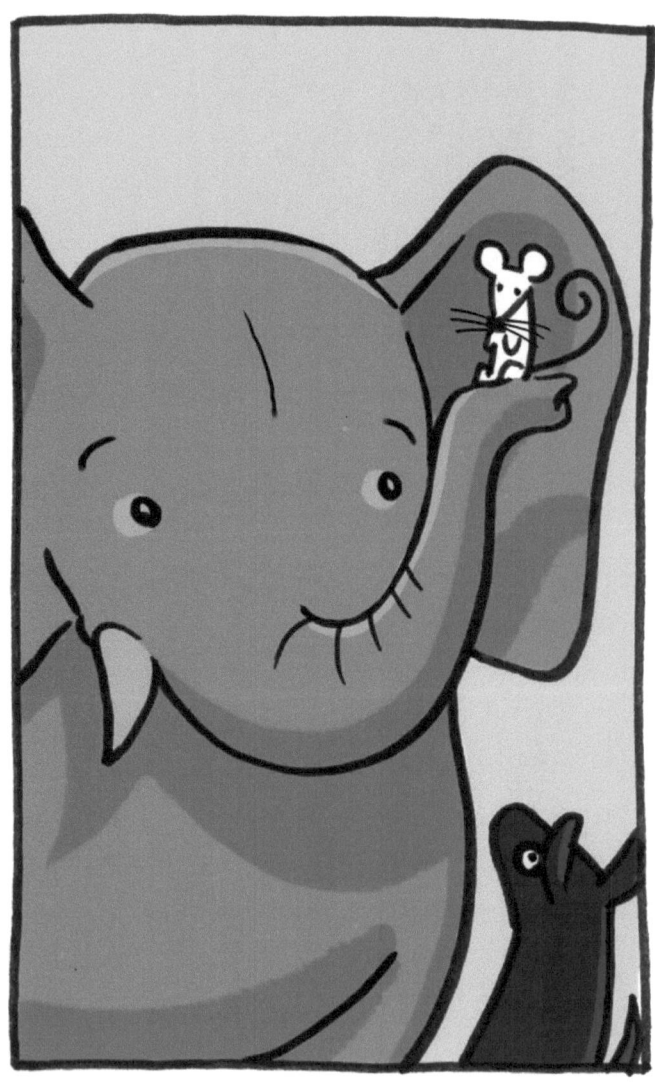

The use of value can be so strong, it can sometimes save a composition that isn't working so well. If you place the lightest light in front of, or next to, the darkest dark, that one spot will pull your viewer's attention right to it. This is like watching a clash of wills, a car accident, or a fight!

Value will also help you hold a shape by contrasting one value against another. For example; a polar bear wouldn't stand out very well in a snowstorm, but if you put a black boat behind him, you could probably just draw his shape, with no features, and your viewer would still know what it is!

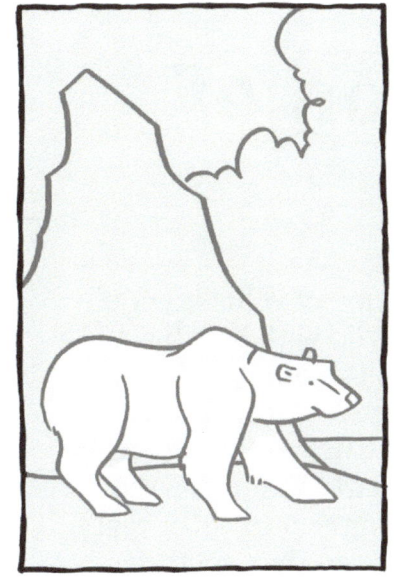 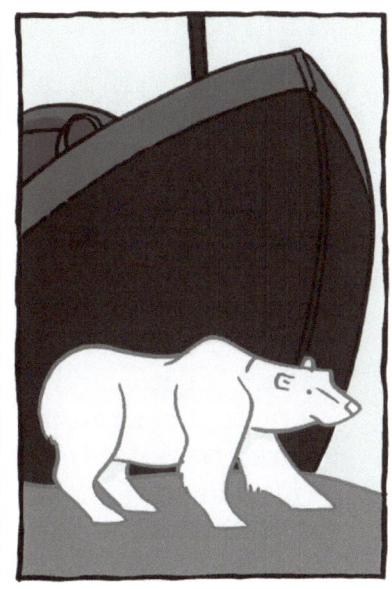

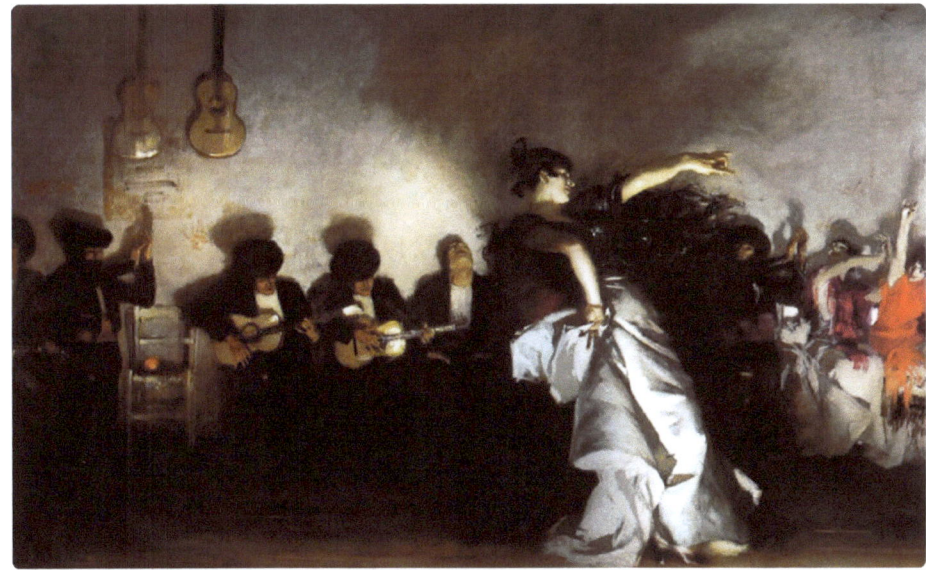

When you do a drawing or painting, use your light very wisely. Where do you want people to look? Whether it is bright sunlight outdoors, or a single light bulb hanging in a darkened room, your light is going to pull your viewer's attention and at the same time, make the objects seem three dimensional.

Example of a Value "fight"
John Singer Sargent, "El Jaleo", 1882 - Isabella Stewart Gardner Museum, Boston, MA, USA

CHAPTER 7

Gradation of Values

A more complex definition of value is equally important, and it has to do with how light affects objects and makes them turn form, or look **three-dimensional**. This light and dark principle is called **Chiaroscuro**, which is Italian for light and dark! When you see a two-dimensional drawing that looks so real it is jumping out of the paper, that is a three dimensional illusion.

There really isn't a three-dimensional object in your sketch book, as each page of your sketchbook is two dimensional, meaning it has height and width. To be three-dimensional (3D), the object must also have depth. Think of a box, or a building!

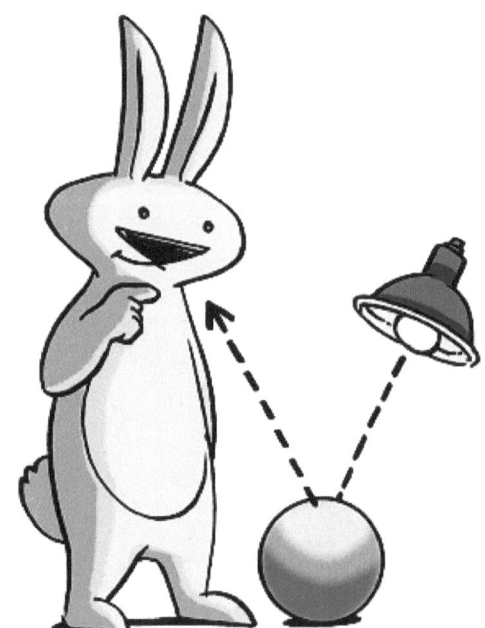
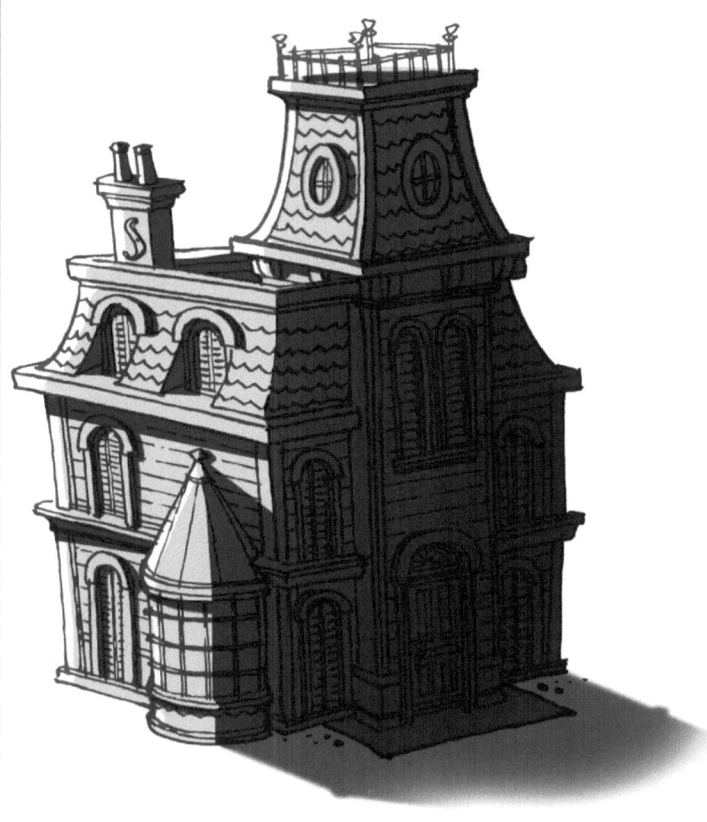

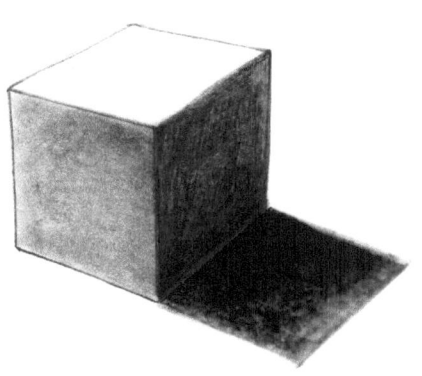

When we talk about value in art, we are sometimes talking about how the light being cast on an object makes it turn form, or look 3D. Without light falling on an object, we can't see that object at all. The very process of seeing anything comes from the light being **refracted**, or bounced back up to our eye, from the object.

As the surface of the object turns away from light and toward the shadow (which is cast by it), it is said to be **turning form**, and it is that gradation of value that makes it look 3D.

Consider a three-dimensional object, such as a white box. A white box will have one side that is the basic value (local value) of the box. Where the light is striking the box directly, it will be lighter, (highlight). Where the box is turning away from the light it will be slightly darker (halftone). And where the light has swept past the box, there will be a cast shadow. That side will mostly be in darkness, but some reflected light will bounce back from the surface the box is sitting on. There is also a core shadow where the halftone and the shadow meet, and a reflected light where the light bounces up onto the box from the surface on which the box is sitting. It might be easier to see the five values on a sphere:

One of the best ways to see this value in light is to put a sphere under a desk lamp. Where the light falls on the sphere, the whole top of the sphere will be what is called **halftone**, or local value (#2), This will be called local color when we start using color. Halftone is the basic value of a flat sphere under light. There will be a very bright spot in the middle of the local value, which is the lightest spot on the sphere. This is the **highlight** (#1). Where the sphere turns from the halftone value to the absence of light, is a dark band, called the **core shadow** (#3). That shadow travels all the way to the underside of the sphere, but it is lit slightly by the light bouncing up from the surface the sphere is resting on. (In color art, the surface under the sphere is also affected by the color of the surface the sphere is resting on.) This is called **reflected light** #4, and is slightly lighter than the core shadow, but not as light as the halftone. Finally, the darkest dark on the object is actually not on the object, but is cast by it. It is the shadow the sphere casts on the surface it is resting on and is called **cast shadow #5.**

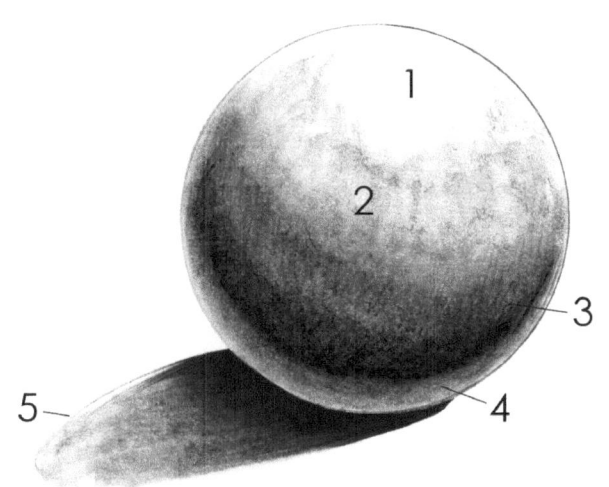

Look at an egg under a light. Where is the darkest spot? Where is the lightest spot? What happens if you move the light away from the egg a little? What happens if you move it very close? What happens to the shadow? You can also try this with different shapes like a white cube (a box), a cylinder (a soup can wrapped in white paper), or something organic in shape and not geometrical, like a person or a pear.

What happens when the object you are looking at is black? Is it the same for any object in a direct light source?

Hard & Soft Edges

There is another major observation at this point, and it is very important for 3D rendering, especially in painting. I am talking about hard edges and soft edges. I know this might seem like a lot to keep track of, but all these rules work together. Edges held with a light against a dark, or dark against light, will have a crisp, or hard, edge. (Remember the fight!) Sides in shadow will melt into the darks around them. These

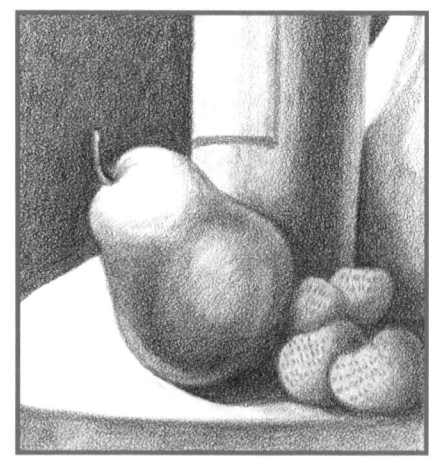

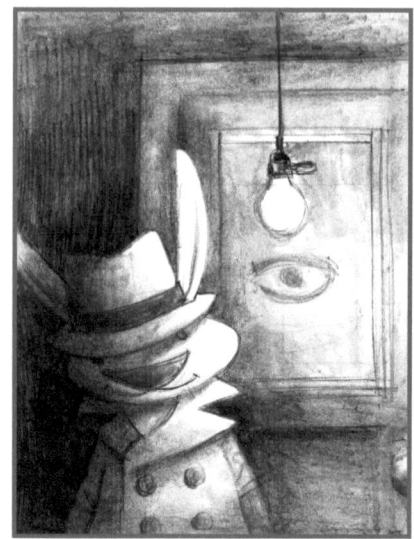

edges will not only make your objects turn form, but will once again help to focus your viewer where you want them to look.

On the next sunny day, go outside and observe your shadow. This is a cast shadow, as opposed to a turning form shadow, and it follows very specific rules. The best way to understand shadows is by observing them at different times of day and in different lighting conditions. Daylight? Artificial light? Spring? Summer? Fall? These will all make your shadow behave differently, but there are some properties that are consistent. The shadow will conform to the rules of perspective, which we will cover later in this book. The shadow will also become more **diffused**, or spread out and less concentrated, the farther it is from the object casting the shadow. A good way to see these two examples is to hold a small lamp over an egg in a semi-dark room. Pull the lamp away from the egg and see the highlight and the shadow become more diffused and less intense.

Bring the lamp closer and the highlight and the shadow become very concentrated and intense.

Go outside at sunrise, at 9:00am, at noon, etc. Look at your cast shadow and at your house's shadow. How do they differ at different times and why?

There is one more trick to use with value- it is the tension and focus that occurs when you put the darkest dark value next to the lightest light, and the hard edge it creates. Combined with a good composition, this one-two punch is irresistible to look at. It pulls the viewer's eye back over and over again! Think about the old coyote silhouette in front of the moon.

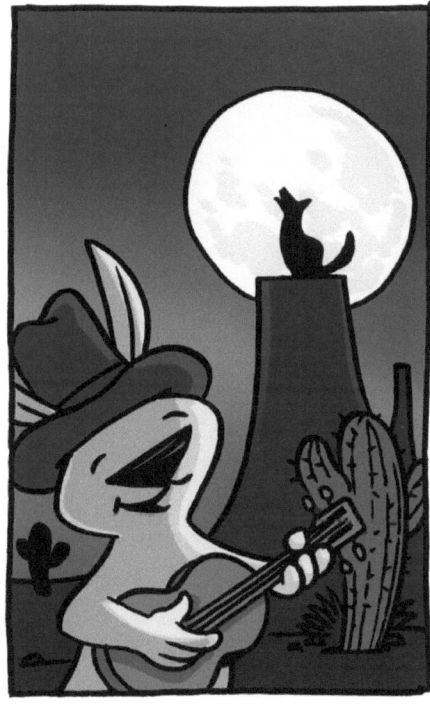

Here is a basic value chart-1 being the lightest to 10 being the darkest. You can see you have ten distinctly different values here.

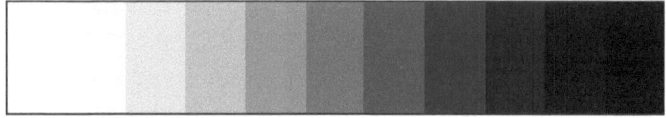

Now, this next part is a very important concept to you as an artist, and as a person, in other situations besides art! What may seem dark to you is only dark in comparison to other values. In other words; a value is only dark or light in relation to other darks or lights. Value, color, size, etc. which are large or small, light or dark, bright or dull, are only judged relative to other elements in a picture.

This seal is the same value in both pictures

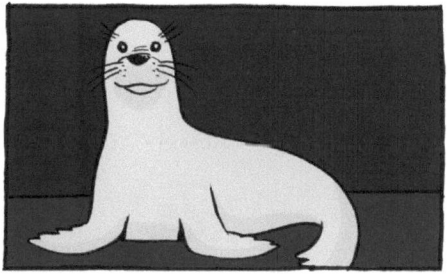
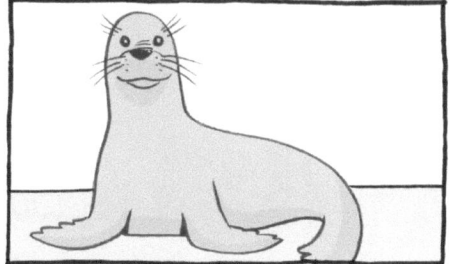

Is a bear large? If you are an ant, a bear is enormous! But what if you are a dragon? Maybe a bear doesn't look so big! The same happens with dark and light. It may be that nighttime is the darkest element in your artwork, or maybe a black tree is silhouetted against a night sky. A polar bear appears white until he is placed against a snow bank, eating a vanilla ice cream cone!

Everything is relative!

You will find examples of this principle in every aspect of your life: rich and poor, fancy and plain, beautiful and ugly, smart or not so smart! To what are you comparing these? things?

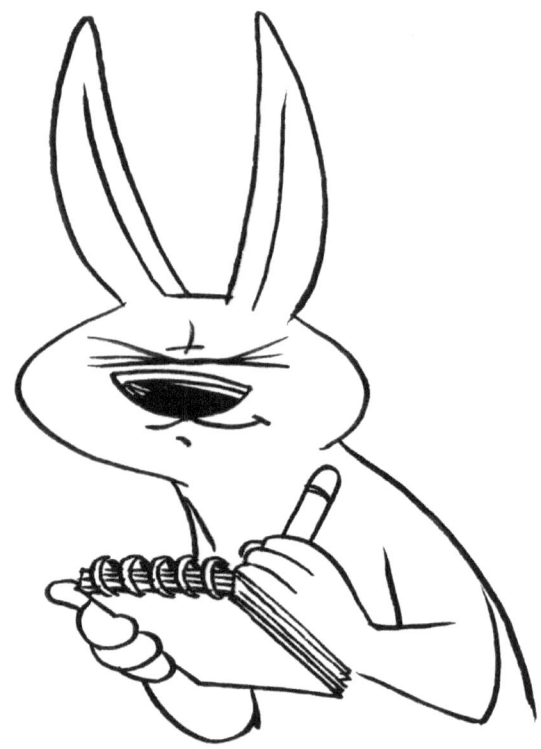

Remember to squint

Squinting is the best way to see the difference in value between two subjects, and the relationships in a composition. Squinting flattens out all the elements so little variations of value in the individual elements don't distract you. In fact, it **posterizes** them, or takes away their three-dimensional qualities so they don't look three-dimensional anymore. The next time you are in a café or grocery store, someplace with windows facing out to the street, stand in the middle of the room, look out the window, and squint.

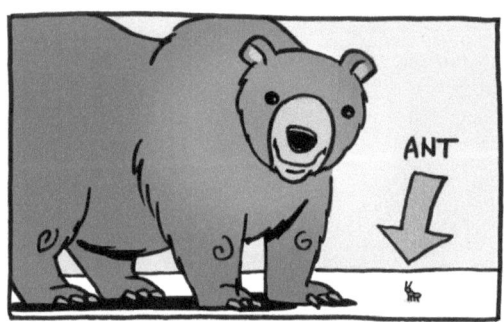
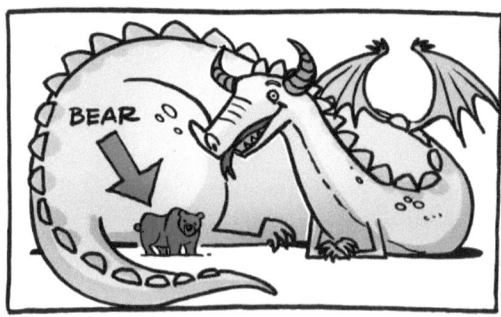

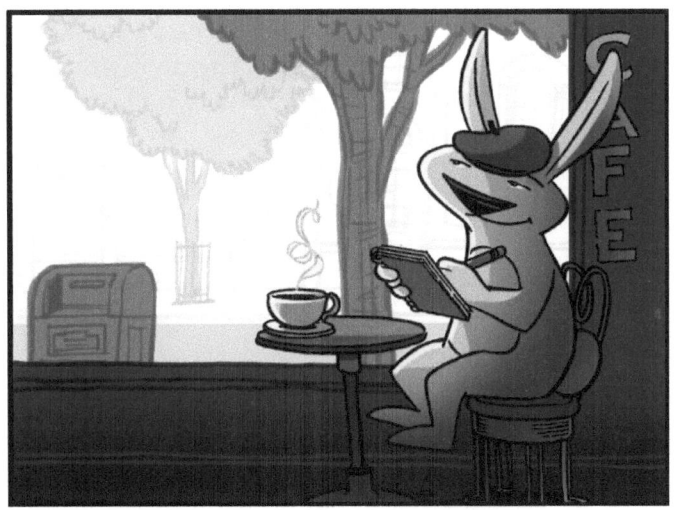

What is the darkest thing in your field of vision? If it is daytime, the darkest object is probably any person or furniture between you and the window. Now find something outside of the window to look at that seems very dark in value. Let's say you spot a tree. Compare the dark of the tree to the person or object between you and the window. The dark object outside the window will be much lighter in value than the person. If you had drawn a picture and made the person lighter, with the tree darker, the distance would look wrong. Every chance you get, **look, compare and remember**. File your observations away in your memory. This will help make you become a better artist, and your work will improve quickly.

See if you can make your own value chart using pencil, charcoal, acrylic, gouache, tempera paint, or watercolor. It's not as easy as you might think, but the more often you do a value chart, the more accurate and the quicker you will become. And as you learn the value changes, you will begin to see the difference between the values in real life and in your artwork. You will have a much better understanding of the slight differences and variations in value.

*Squint at your chart.
Do you see any jumps
(abrupt changes) between the values?*

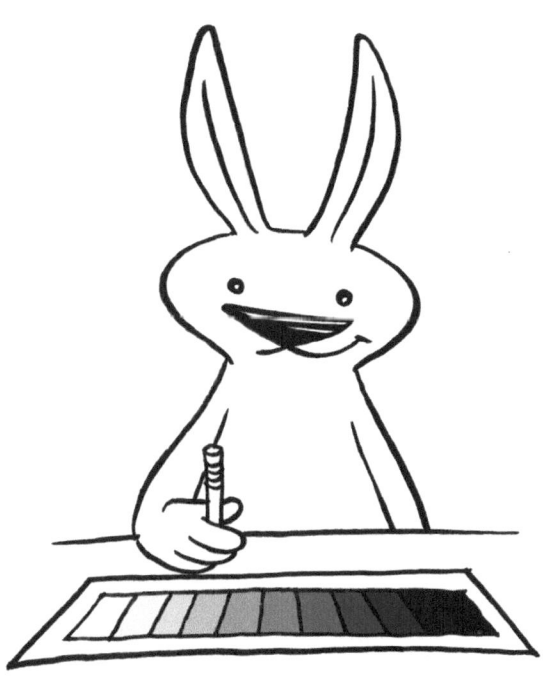

These are huge considerations for your work, so again, this would be a wonderful time to take a look at some of your art to see if you can apply value improvements. If you drew something that should be turning form, and it isn't as successful as you think it could be, maybe you can find that object, try lighting it, and observe it, to better achieve that goal. You could also take this opportunity to make your drawing more dramatic by "punching up" the contrast- in other words, change the values or value relationships. Squint at these!

Famous artist's use of contrasting value, and blending of values

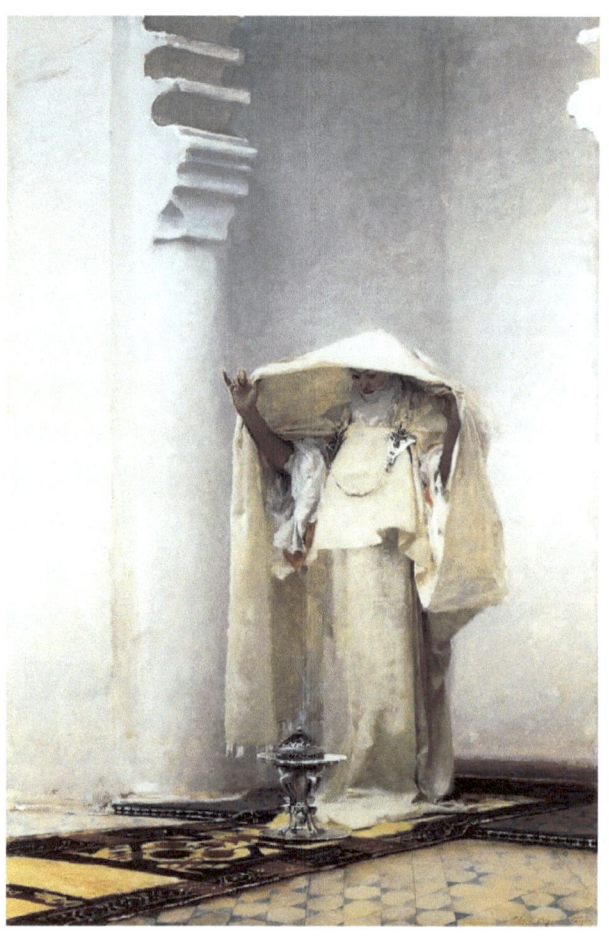
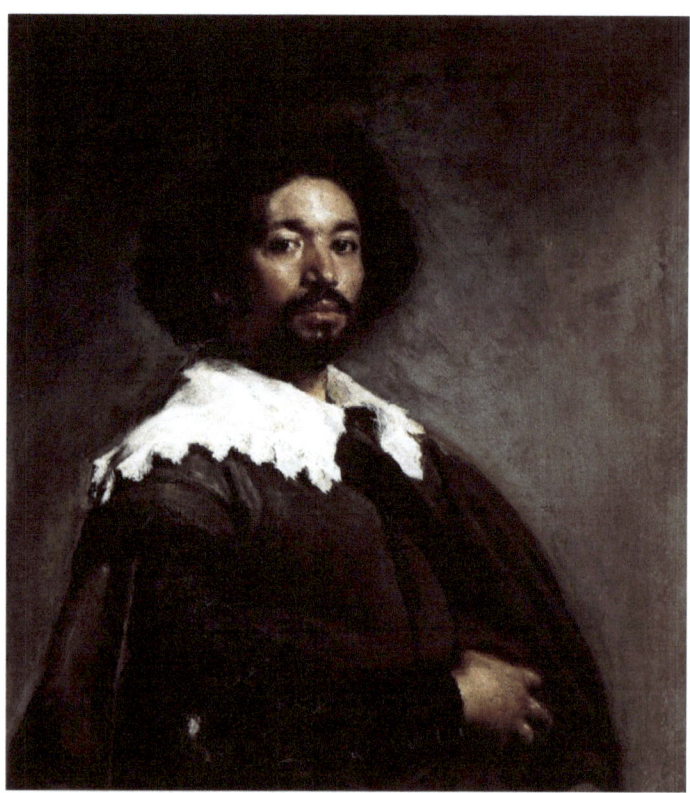

Left to Right: John Singer Sargent, Fumee d'Ambre Gris, 1880, Clark Art Institute / **Velasquez, Juan de Pareja**, 1650, Metropolitan Museum of Art

CHAPTER 8
Tension

Another possibility that can make your composition more exciting is turning the balance around and creating an imbalance of sorts. In a cartoon, when a character like Wile E. Coyote is trying to catch the Road Runner (yet again), he might suspend a huge weight like a piano or a safe over the Road Runner's head. That creates **tension** for the viewer. It immediately makes the viewer sit up and pay attention, with a feeling that something is going to happen. Your art piece can do the same thing, but it doesn't have to be as literal as the Road Runner cartoons!

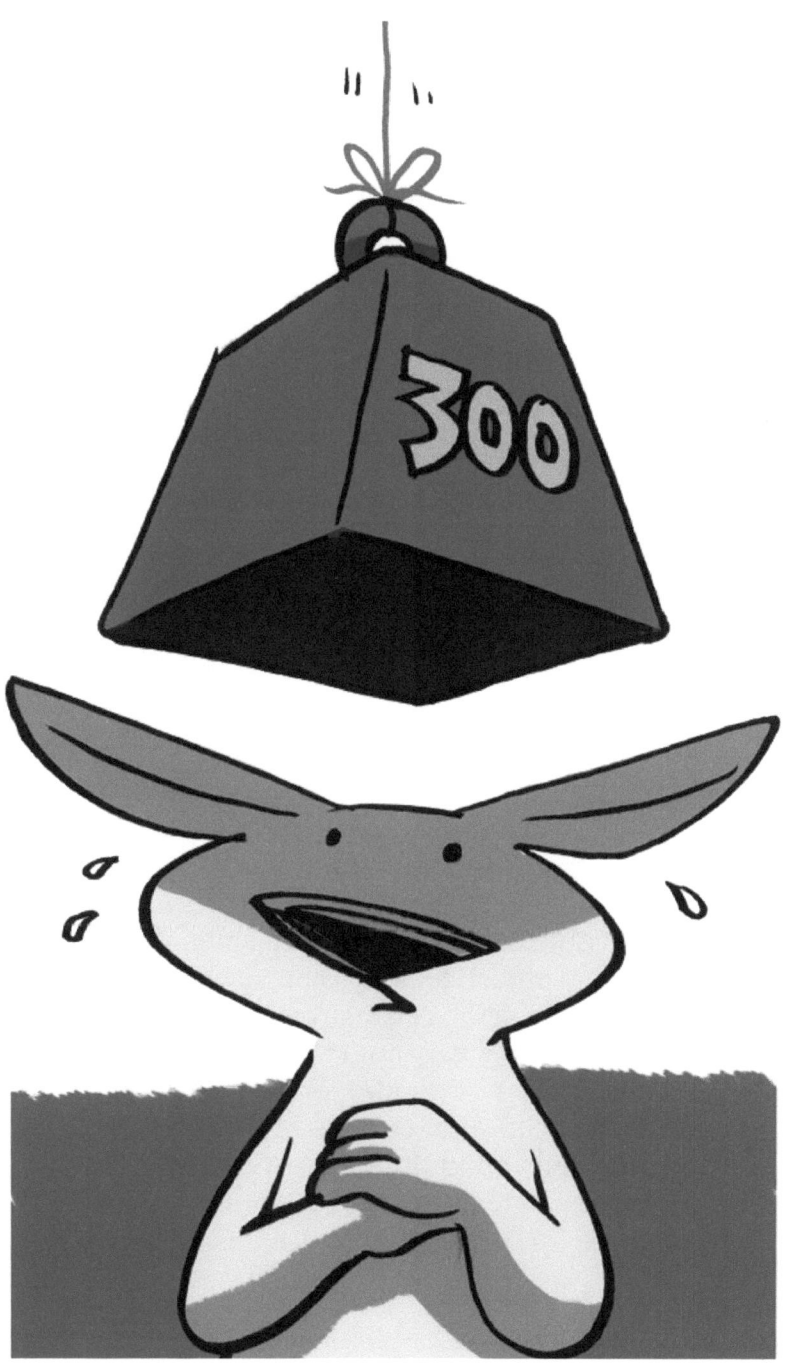

Three more attention grabbers

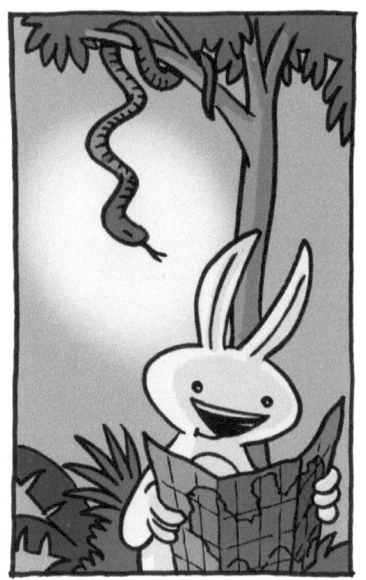
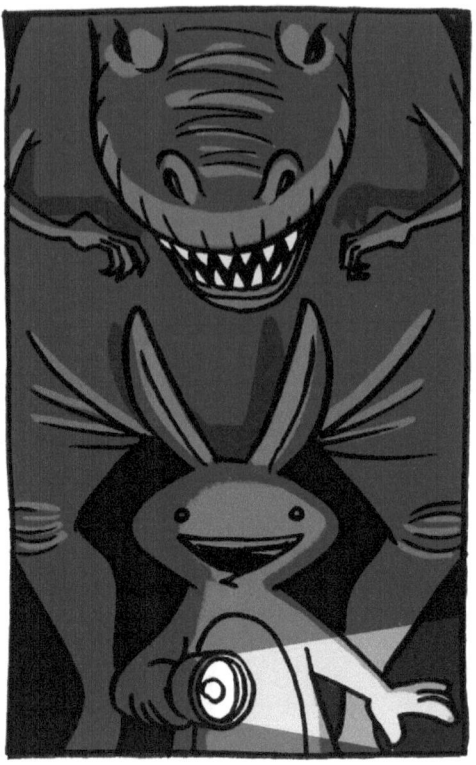
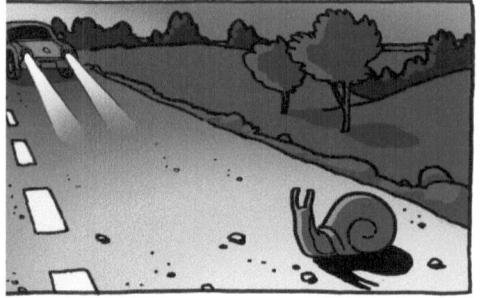

Tension can simply be the use of a visual trick to present a combination, or situation, which is obviously wrong. It could be a large pointed object dangling above a small or vulnerable object, a mouse chasing a lion, a compressed spring getting ready to jump, someone getting very angry and red-faced (getting ready to explode), or a snail crossing a highway with a car coming in the distance. It can be tension in the story, or just an uneasy visual tension. Let's see what Murphy can come up with!

Details in and out of focus

We have talked a lot about varying the value of different elements in your piece, about hierarchy of size, and even about having different edges. Here is another trick to go with that set of possibilities. You can focus attention on what you want to stand out by making your main object have a highly detailed rendering, and not including as much detail in any of your other elements. The viewer's eye will go to the detail first, and will fill in the rest of the picture's details in their brain. Try this experiment: sit or stand straight up, facing an object in your room. Stare at the object straight on and don't move your eyes. How much detail can you see in that object? Quite a bit, I bet. In fact, as long as your vision is good, you can see all of it clearly.

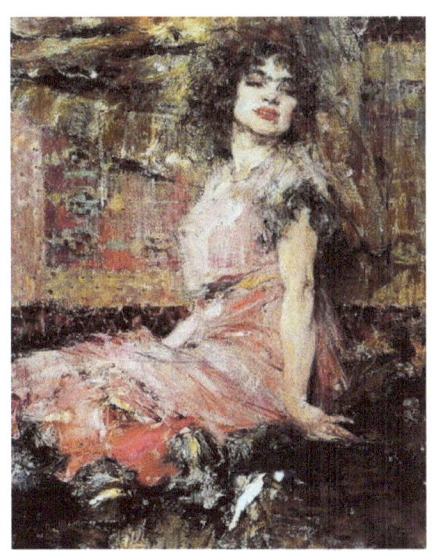

Nicolai Fechin, "Lady in Pink (Portrait of Natalia Podbelskaya)", 1912, Frye Art Museum

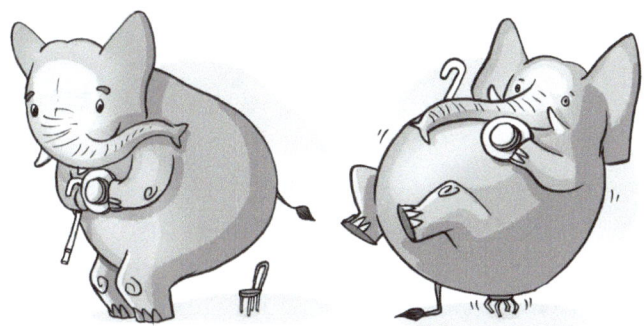

Now don't move your eyes, but see if you can see any other objects around or near that object you are focused on. This is called using your peripheral vision. You can see other objects nearby, but unless you move your eyes, you can't see them in any detail. This is one way you can develop your art piece. If you put the same detail everywhere, the viewer's eye won't know what to look at first. Try combining this with sweet spots and value to reinforce the focus. You can't lose! How can you use these suggestions to improve your work?

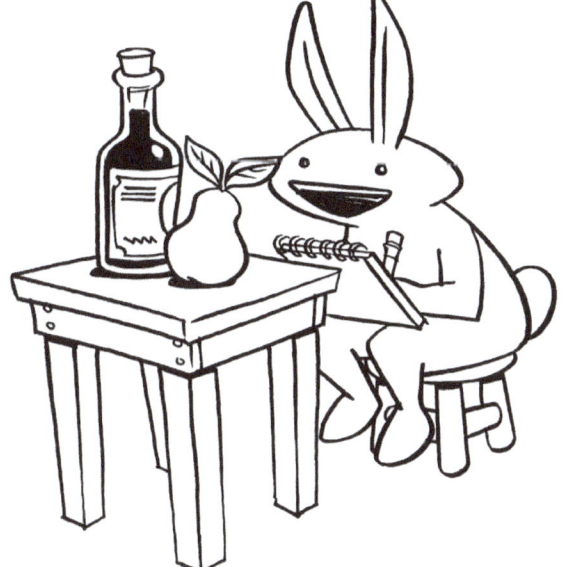

Tension can also come from anticipation of a near-future event. In this example, the elephant on the left is hovering over a tiny chair. The elephant's weight is distributed in such a way that we are pretty sure the chair is not going to fare well from the encounter. The elephant on the right has sat on the chair which is straining under its weight. Although this second elephant is funny, it only works because we set up the scene with the previous image. Otherwise, it would be hard to read what is happening. The "sweeter" of the two frozen moments is the elephant on the left. Although the moment is static, we are entertained by the anticipation and building tension of future events, even if we will never actually see the outcome.

CHAPTER 9
Texture & Pattern

You may notice another strong compositional element in famous works of art, and that is the use of texture and pattern. You see it in photography, paintings, movies, games, and advertising. You will see the use of **Pattern** and **Texture** just about everywhere in art because it is everywhere in life. Can you remember the movie The Wizard of Oz? One of the famous scenes shows Dorothy in a field of poppies, and as the camera pulls back, the little figure of Dorothy pops right out, because she is not part of the pattern. (This is also a very interesting perspective for the composition, but we will get to that in the perspective chapter!) Texture or pattern used in this way is like a bonus value. You can use it to define a shape or a background, as you would with a different value. It makes the composition more interesting as well because the eye has something else, or something different to look at.

Artists have made series of work based just on repeating patterns, with either slight or complete changes to the pattern as their focal point. Take a look at this example!

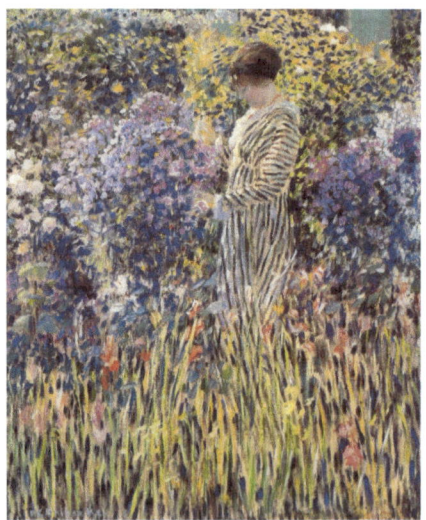 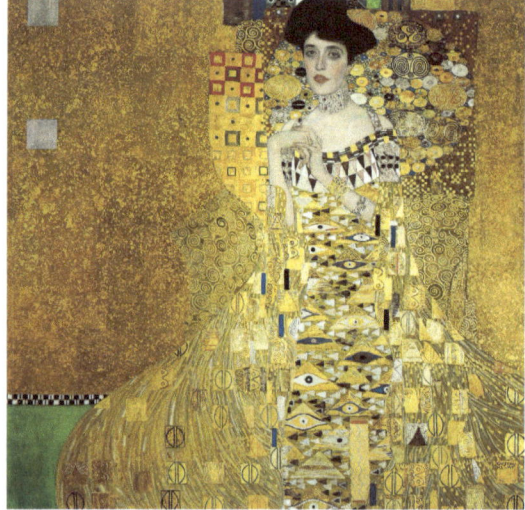

Frederick Carl Frieseke, *Lady in the Garden, 1915 - Terra Foundation for American Art, Daniel J. Terra Collection* / ***Gustav Klimt***, *Portrait of Adele Bloch-Bauer, Neue Galerie, New York*

MONOCHROME WITH COLOR ACCENTS

Here is an idea that has worked well for artists since ancient art was first painted on cave walls. Though many artists, past and present have used this design technique, we will use one master illustrator for our example, and that master is Howard Pyle. He used a very simple design method on many of his book illustrations. Many of his books dealt with history, particularly pirates and soldiers. This technique uses **Monochrome** images (which means one color) and in this case, black on white. The trick is to add one small spot of color, which pulls the viewer's attention right to that spot! Howard Pyle frequently used the color red for these accents. In fact, sometimes even when he worked in color, he would only really use a subdued palette, or set of colors, almost monochrome, and use that flash of red only for emphasis. Below are some examples of how that can work:

In a future book about color, we will talk about accenting a warm color in an all cool painting, or the other way around. That trick will work in full color as well as one in a monochrome system. One caution though; this is a time when your value pattern must be very clear and effective, or your accent may fight with your intention. How can these aspects of pattern and accents help improve your drawings?

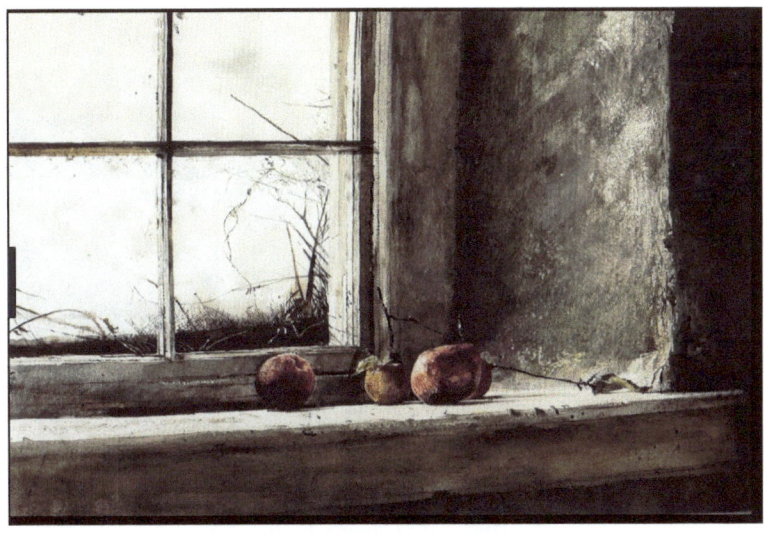 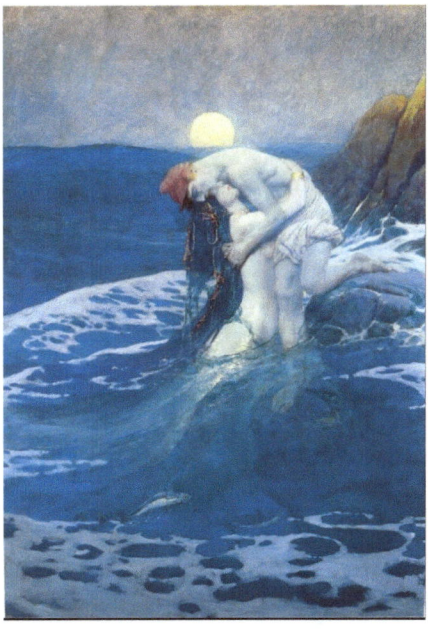

Andrew Wyeth, "Frostbitten", 1962, National Gallery / **N.C. Wyeth**, "The Mermaid" - 1910 - Delaware Art Museum

CHAPTER 10
Perspective

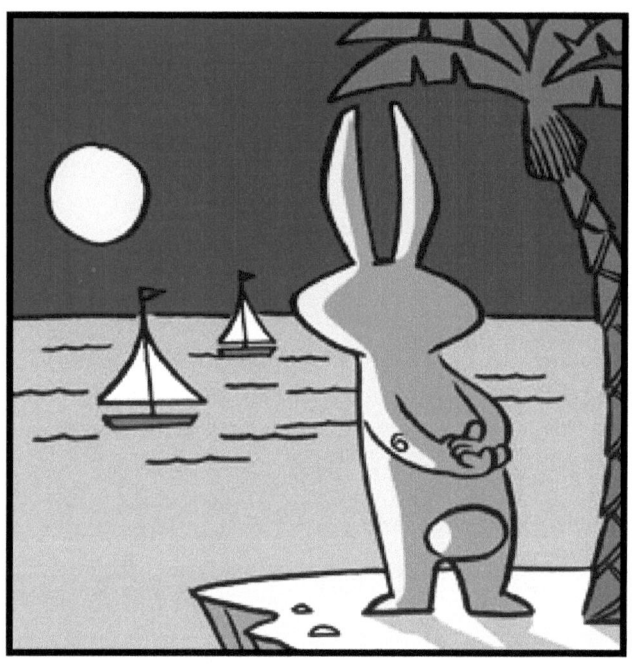

When you look out to sea, do you ever notice that line on the horizon? Well, that is called the **"Horizon Line"**. It is where the land meets the sky, and it is the horizontal origin of all **Perspective** lines.

The horizon line represents where your viewer's eye is located in relation to the subject within your drawing. Here, the horizon line is at the same 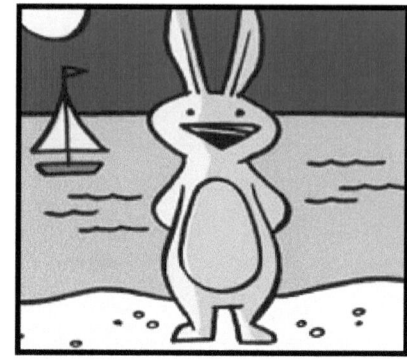 level as Murphy's eyes. This means that the viewer's eyes are at the same height as Murphy's.

Where the horizon line is located in your picture tells the viewer where he is in relation to the subject. A low Horizon Line means you are below the subject. A high horizon line means you are above the subject.

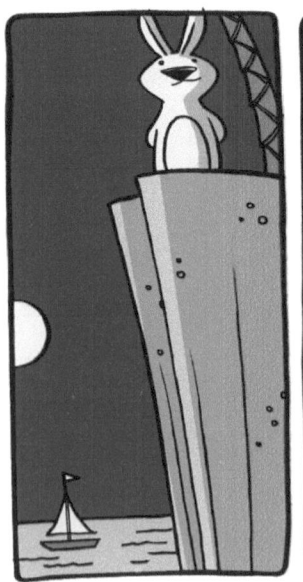 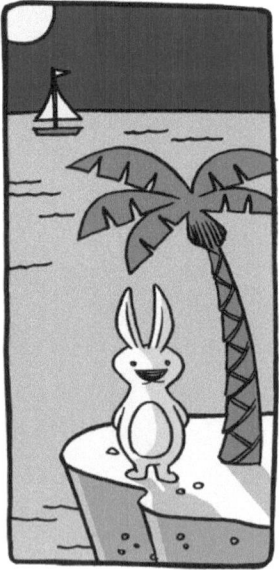

Objects in your picture are also affected by their location in relation to the Horizon Line. In these examples the Horizon Line is located in the middle of the picture.

Although the drawing is flat, the box we are depicting is dimensional, and follows the rules of Perspective.

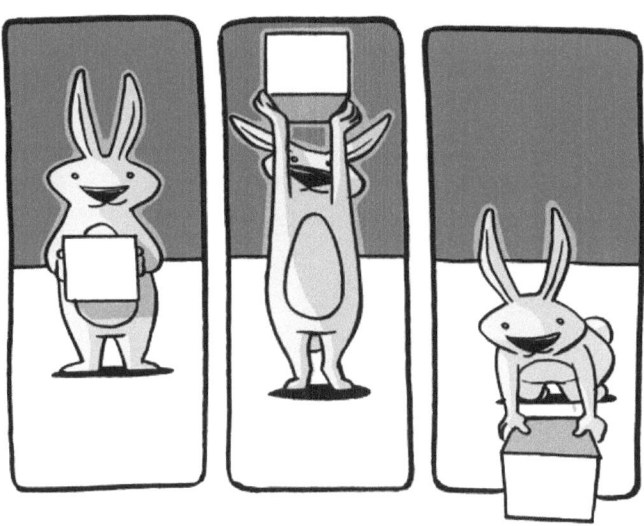

So, where an object is, in relation to the Horizon Line, tells you whether you can see the top or bottom of that object-even with circular objects like the plates in the image below.

No matter the shape, the horizon line tells the viewer where they are in relation to the objects and subjects in your pictures.

1. Murphy is holding a box. When the box is placed right in front of the Horizon Line you can see the front of the box, but not the top or bottom. (Remember, your viewer's eyes are even with the horizon line.)

2. When he holds the box above the Horizon Line you can see the bottom of the box.

3. When he holds the box below the Horizon Line you can see the top of the box.

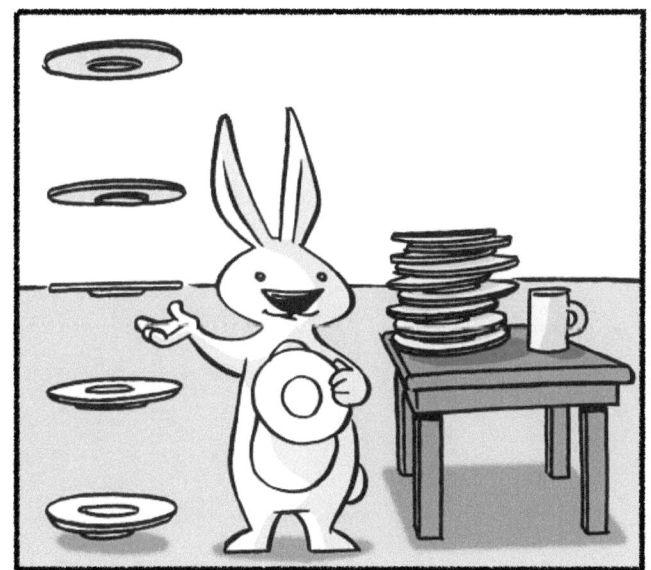

VANISHING POINT

When you draw an object or environment in Perspective, not only does the Horizon Line describe what part of the object you see, but those objects and details will also get smaller the farther away they are from you. Along that line is a point called the Vanishing Point. This is the point where your viewer's eye location intersects with the horizon.

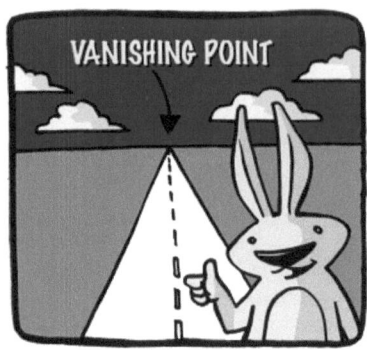

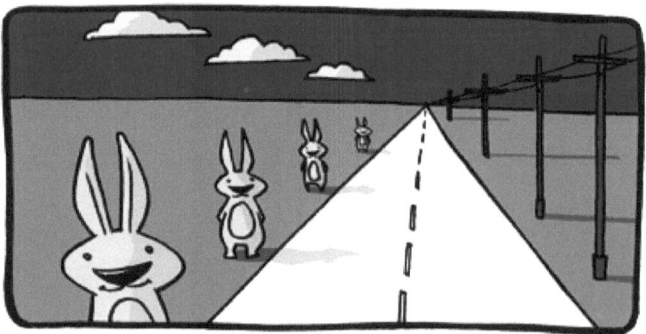

Perspective is a lot like a road. Along this road objects get smaller as they get closer to the horizon line's vanishing point.

Just like the lines of that road, all objects get smaller as they get closer to the Vanishing Point. Notice that these lines also help you know what sides of an object you will see as it recedes towards the Horizon Line.

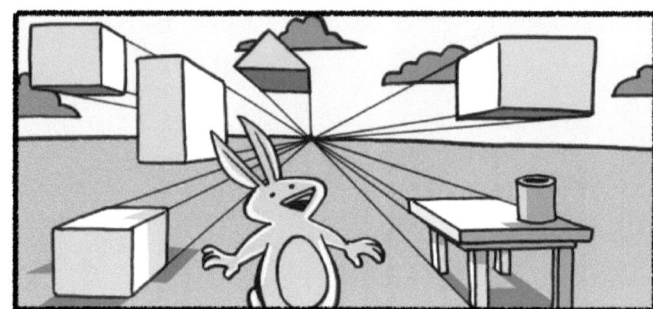

The Vanishing Point can appear anywhere along the Horizon Line, and affects all objects, no matter how big or small they might be. Below is an example of One-Point Perspective.

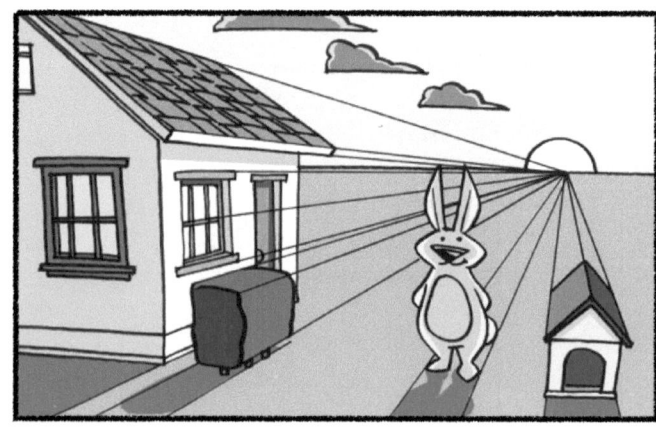

This is a very brief introduction to the basic rules of Perspective, but it is far from all there is to know. Whole books have been written on the subject of Perspective, so for now we encourage you to play with these ideas. study other artist's work and see how they have used these rules of Perspective to add depth to their artwork.

PERSPECTIVE & LIGHT

When it come to light in your picture, shadows follow the same rules as perspective lines, with the light source acting as its own vanishing point. The location of a light source will not affect the perspective lines in your picture, but drawing lines to your light source will help you figure out where the shadows of the objects in your picture will fall.

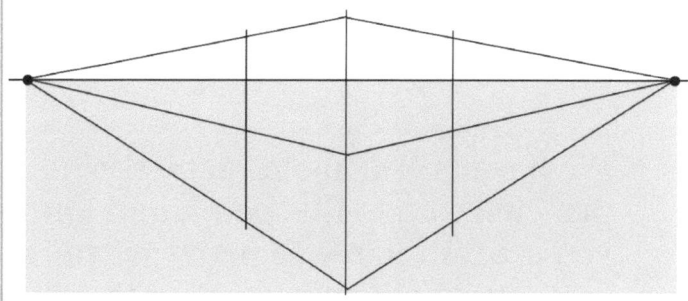

TWO-POINT PERSPECTIVE

If an object can be seen from two sides at once, each of those sides disappear to a Vanishing Point on the horizon. This is called Two-Point Perspective. These points may go very far to the right and left, and may even go outside of your format, but the principle is still there. When drawing a head from a 3/4 view, that same perspective principle will apply, with a front plane and a side plane being visible.

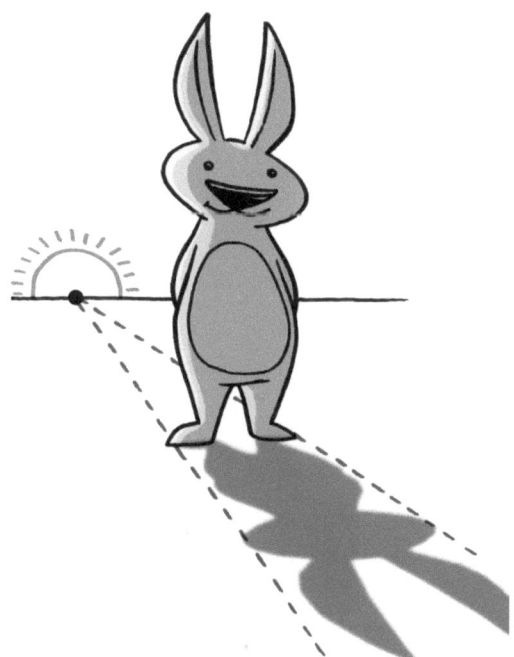

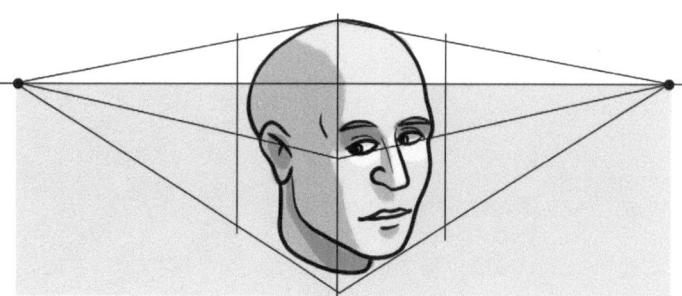

CHAPTER 11
Story & Opinion

We have talked about many design principles up to this point, and I am sure you are familiar with many artists, not just the artists we have used as examples in this book. They have solved many visual problems in very many ways. Did they all solve the same problems in the same way? I hope not! The world would need only one artist if all artists saw the world in the same way. It would be like eating the same dinner every night for your entire life.

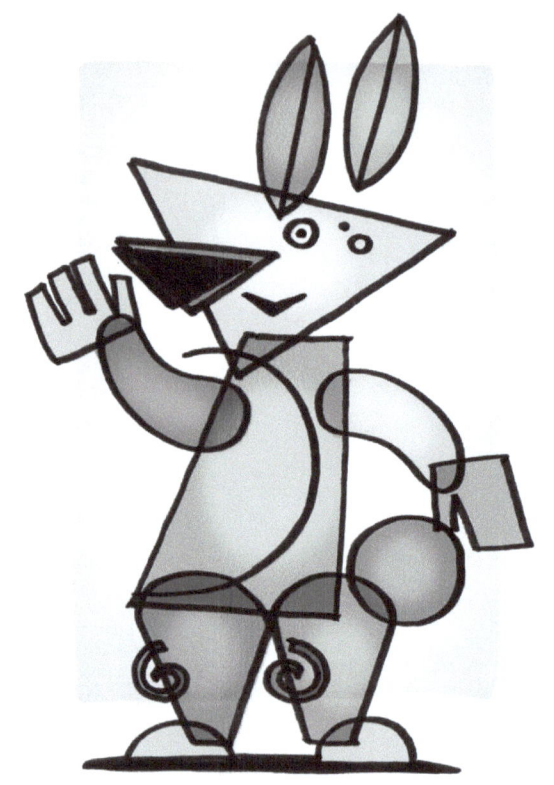

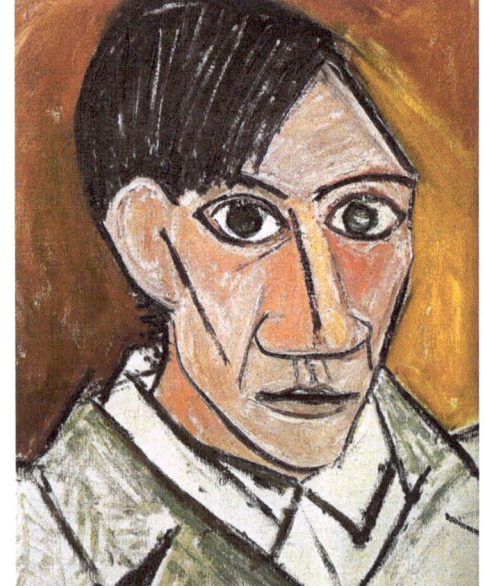

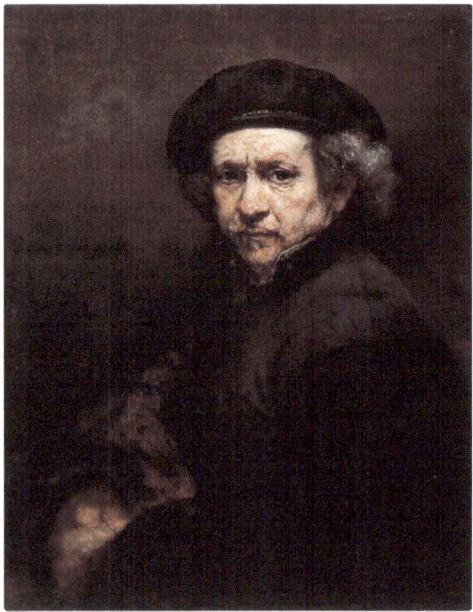

Pablo Picasso, Self-Portrait, 1907 - Narodni Galerie, Prague, Czech Republic,

Rembrandt, Self-Portrait, 1659 - National Gallery

Have a look at how the same artist, Pablo Picasso, chose to depict a figure in two very different portraits:

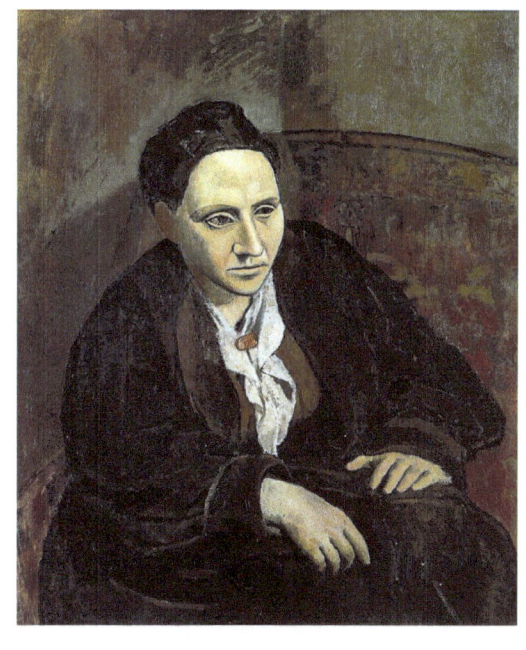

This is what makes you unique as an artist. Your opinion matters very much, and no one else will ever have the same exact approach, or style, as you. As you become more comfortable with your art form, all of these rules will become part of your subconscious, the part of your thinking that is automatic. You don't have to think about walking or breathing, and soon, you won't have to think about drawing or designing either. You will sense when something is right or wrong, and if it's wrong, then you will have the tools to analyze and correct the problem.

Pablo Picasso, Gerturde Stein, 1906 - Metropolitan Museum of Art, New York City,

Pablo Picasso, Dora Maar, 1941 - Private Collection

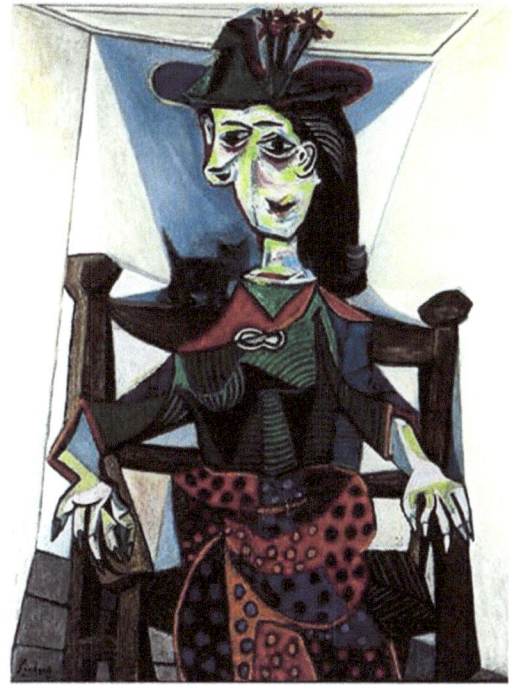

These artists all represented a vase of flowers in entirely different ways.

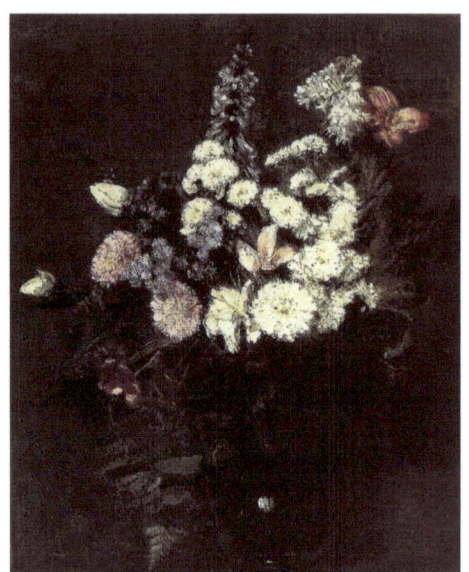
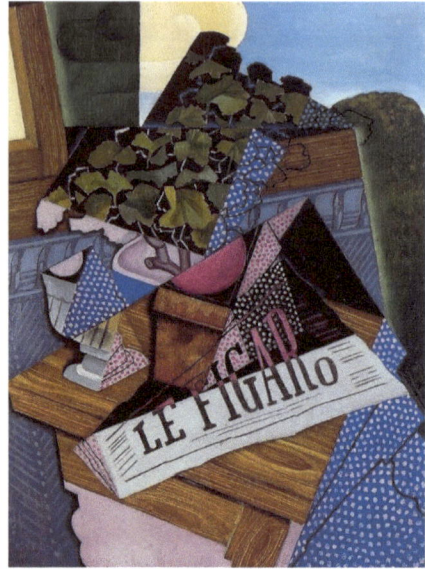
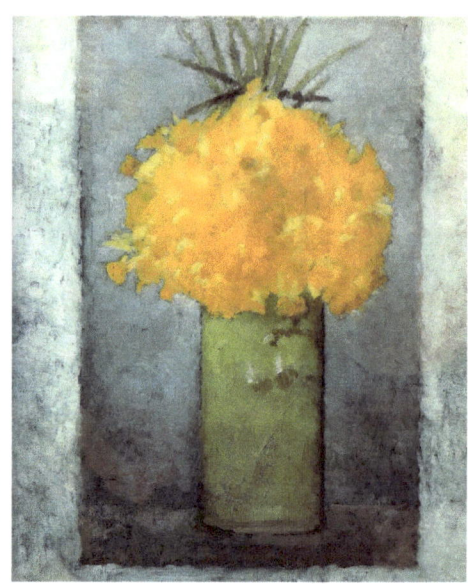
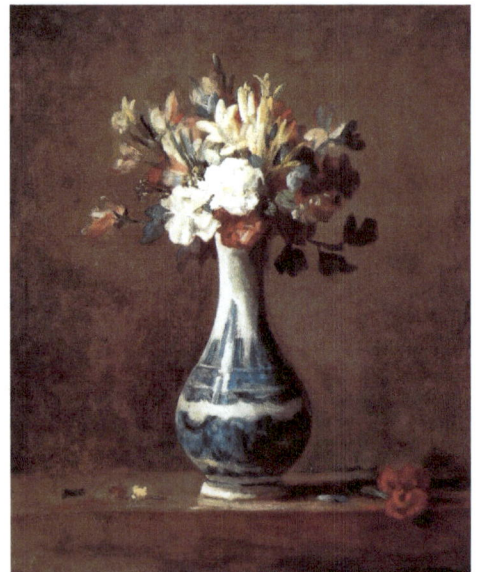

Henri Fantin-Latour, Autumn Flowers, 1861 - Private Collection / **Juan Gris**, A Pot of Geraniums, 1915 - Private Collection / **Pierre Bonnard**, Daffodils in a Green Pot, 1867 - Private Collection / **Jean-Baptiste-Simeon Chardin**, Still Life Flowers in Vase, 1763 - National Gallery of Scotland,

If you are familiar with these artists, you will recognize their work immediately when you see it. That is because these artists all had an opinion about a vase of flowers, and about painting in general. Artists often have strong opinions about a subject. Let's take the subject of a country's revolution for example. Compare the patriotic reverence of Howard Pyle's American Revolution paintings, to Jacque-Louis David's vision of the death of his heroic Marat Sade in the French revolution, and Picasso's depiction of the Spanish revolution, in one of the most powerful murals of all time, called simply Guernica. These are three very different opinions, or way of visualizing, the same subject.

These last three paintings have one characteristic they all share-all three paintings follow a story. The traditional art form that concerns itself with story is called illustration, but there is a very fine line between illustration and fine art. You will find a storyline in most art, with the exception of pure design using form or color, like the works of Mondrian or Albers. Some artists make it harder to spot the story, like Jackson Pollack, or Franz Kline, but not being in the artist's mind, I wouldn't rule it out. Even still lives, or landscapes, tell a story about time of day, seasonal light, wealth or poverty, neatness or clutter, and so on. Animators and movie set designers must concern themselves with the story first. Photographers sometimes see the story after the photograph materializes on the monitor screen or the paper. The most important aspect of the story is the continuous support of the main theme. Contradictions in the story of a painting become confusing. If you are observing and representing an opulent villa in Europe, and your story is about how rich and cultured the subject is, you wouldn't include a pile of garbage in the front yard, even if you see it.

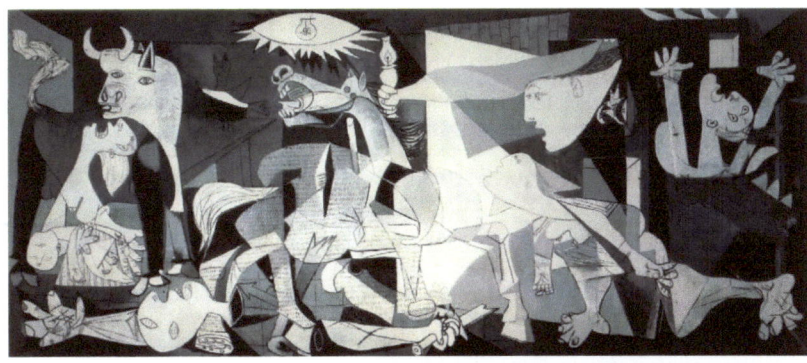

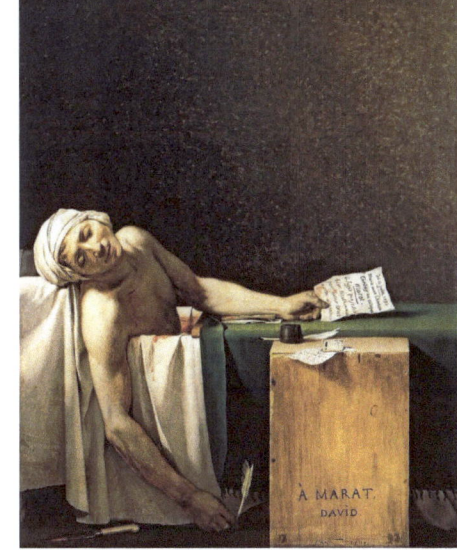

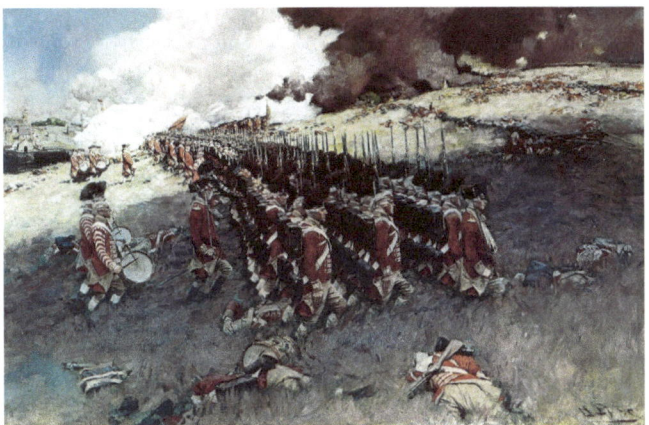

Pablo Picasso, "Guernica", 1937 - Museo Reina Sofia, Madrid, Spain / **Jacques-Louis David**, "The Death of Marat", 1793 - Musées Royaux des Beaux Arts, Brussels, Belgium / **Howard Pyle**, "Battle of Bunker Hill", 1897 - Delaware Art Museum (missing presumed stolen)

That would change the theme of the story. So remember if you are out painting **"en plein air"**, (outside on location), and you are making a painting of a villa in Europe, and there is a pile of garbage in the front yard, you could choose to omit that. You could also choose to leave it in, but be aware, you are creating a different story, which may be just what you want. If you paint the old man down the street, and you like the old man, your story about him will be different than the story your next door neighbor may paint, if they are not sympathetic to the old man. Stories and opinions vary from artist to artist, depending on the artists' experiences. Just make sure, if you compose a painting that tells a story, that all of the elements in your painting support the story you want to tell.

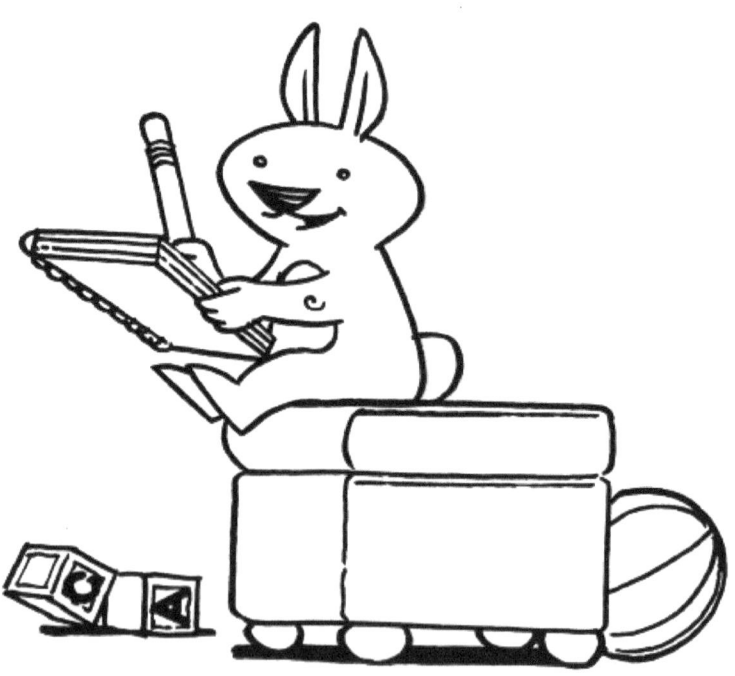

Conclusion

Murphy has demonstrated many important design concepts for the training artist. Some will be more important to you than others. Are you a Sargent? A Picasso? A Bonnard? A Wyeth? Or unlike any artist that has come before? You may decide to break all these rules, and that is your choice, because you are the artist. You are in control of your creations. Your praise or criticism will depend on your choices, but it really doesn't matter, as long as you are pleased with your journey. However, these concepts will help you accomplish the art you want to make, and they will help you to critique, or analyze your own work.

It may seem like there are too many rules to remember, while you work on your pieces, but eventually, all of those possibilities will become part of you and you won't have to think about them anymore. They will become like musical scales to a musician. Sometimes you may not understand one or even all of these principles, but if you keep on practicing, and doing your art, all of a sudden you will find yourself saying " OH! That's what that means!" These realizations will often come to you when you are the most frustrated. Why is that? Because you have improved and are just ready to jump up to the next level. You recognize now that something is wrong, but you don't know what it is. Only someone who ceases to strive thinks themselves unable to improve. You may make one of these revelations 10 years down the road, or maybe more! Keep drawing, painting, weaving, photographing, sculpting, or whatever your chosen art medium. Don't become discouraged if you can't produce exactly what you want right away. Every art form needs practice. One can't be Rembrandt overnight! I had a sculpting teacher who said it took 50 head sculptures to know how to sculpt a head, and that every artist has 10,000 bad drawings in them- so get them out of the way, as fast as you can!

ABOUT THE AUTHOR

Nadya Geras-Carson started with a BFA in Theatre Arts and then earned another BFA in Illustration. She worked as a Dimensional Designer, and Concept Painter for Walt Disney Imagineering. Because of the sculpting experience at WDI, Nadya turned to studying classical sculpture as well as painting. She now works and teaches in Eugene, Oregon where she lives with her husband, designer and artist Don Carson, and various critters.

www.ingramcontent.com/pod-product-compliance
Lightning Source LLC
Chambersburg PA
CBHW051216220526
45473CB00003B/1062